Handbook for Trauma **Survivors**

Empowering Recovery:
Practical Strategies for Healing from Trauma

Written by Trauma Survivor, Myra Abrams

First published in Far North Queensland, 2024 by Bowerbird Publishing

@ 2024 Myra Abrams

The moral rights of the author have been asserted. All rights reserved. Except as permitted under the Australian Copyright Act 1968 (for example, a fair dealing for the purposes of study, research, criticism or review), no part of this book may be reproduced,stored in a retrieval system, communicated or transmitted in any form or by any means without prior written permission. All enquiries should be made to the author.

ISBN 978-1-7635642-3-6 (paperback)
ISBN 978-1-7635642-4-3 (ebook)

Handbook for Trauma Survivors
Empowering Recovery: Practical Strategies for Healing from Trauma
Myra Abrams

First edition: 2024

Edited by: Crystal Leonardi, Bowerbird Publishing
Interior Design by: Crystal Leonardi, Bowerbird Publishing
Front Cover Design: Crystal Leonardi, Bowerbird Publishing

Distributed by Bowerbird Publishing
Available in National Library of Australia

Disclaimer: The material in this publication is of the nature of general comment only, and does not represent professional advice. It is not intended to provide specific guidance for particular circumstances and it should not be relied on as the basis of any decision to take action or not take action on any matter which it covers. Readers should obtain professional advice where appropriate, before making any such decision. To the maximum extent permitted by law, the author and publisher disclaim all responsibility and liability to any person, arising directly or indirectly from any person taking or not taking action based on the information in this publication.

Bowerbird Publishing
Julatten, Queensland, Australia
www.crystalleonardi.com

This book is dedicated to all trauma survivors,
affirming their right to seek assistance.

It serves as a guide on the journey toward
deeper self-understanding. I encourage you to avail yourself
of professional support and utilize the strategies outlined in this handbook
to facilitate your quest.

✫

FOREWORD

What an incredible resource this handbook is for people grappling with the devastating impacts of childhood trauma.

The author has done a remarkable job summing up in a profound way the various stages of the healing journey and how therapeutic strategies support each step.

Survivors are invited to begin their own personal journey of healing, wherever they're at. Whether you're still grappling to comprehend your trauma or if you're in the thick of processing memories or healing generational wounds, anyone can utilise the skills and knowledge in this handbook for their recovery.

The vast amount of literature and concepts discussed with relevant links to academic and credible sources makes this Handbook a reliable source for survivors on the road to healing.

The easy-to-use worksheets, journal prompts and thought-provoking questions encourage survivors to lean into their personal work and feel supported.

The list of regional and nationwide trauma informed supports is comprehensive and vital for supporting survivors who regionally cannot access local support services.

To all fellow survivors, I wish you all the very best on your path to healing. You deserve to be supported on this journey. Never forget that the work you do on yourself is the most valuable work you will ever do. I hope that this hand book is a valuable tool for your healing and for your life.

- Imogen

ABOUT THE AUTHOR

Our lifetime of trauma began at 22-months of age. This was when we lost our HOST (the person we were born as) to extreme trauma. FINAL OBLIVION is the complete and permanent disappearance or cessation of a particular alter personality. At 3-years of age, Aimee is an 'old soul' and became HOST #2 and so Dissociative Identity Disorder (DID) began.

The thing about complex traumas is that some of the personalities the brain creates as a reaction to the trauma, can be different from the HOST. However, we didn't know this. The brain keeps everything a big secret, which decreases the sense of self.

Here is a poem we wrote in 2012 explaining how it feels to not know who you are...

Who Am I?
It's the words over and over and over and over and over and over and over again. ENDLESSLY. All crazy. All crazy as all hell breaking loose.
Came and came and came and came to a puzzled place.

When we reached 4-years of age, when a healthy child's sense of self is developing, we had 31 personalities. This means the ego had split into 31 parts or segments, like a mandarin fruit.

Not everyone who reads this handbook has complex trauma. Some may have had a more recent trauma, such as a car accident or being caught in a natural disaster. Some may have come from a war zone. In these cases, you may lose your sense of self because the incident has removed you from your life and put you in a situation where you feel a loss of control. This is a truly horrible situation, that can go on indefinitely, triggering anxiety or panic attacks. Traumas have the power to change your life path if given permission.

The strategies in this book are for anyone who has experienced trauma at any time in their lives. If I had had a resource like this when I was younger, it would have helped immensely.

I hope it starts you on a journey of self-discovery, including finding a professional therapist. We, personally, have seen 17 therapists in Victoria, New South Wales and Queensland. They all had different idiosyncrasies that detracted from the client/therapist relationship. For example, in Victoria, we had a therapist who fell asleep in our session. The house cat came and sat on our lap, and we watched the therapist until he awoke. We didn't go back. We found another who treated us like a specimen. We didn't go back.

Good luck with your journey. Never give up, and remember it is your right to move on until you find a professional who has strong therapeutic boundaries and is a good reflective listener. You want someone who validates what you are telling her/him. This is the beginning of your journey. Go well, fellow traveller.

To contact the author, email: traumahandbook2024@gmail.com

AUTHOR'S NOTE

I highly recommend writing down your notes and beliefs in a notebook or scrapbook that you can take to therapy. The things you write are your journey notes and in them will be things to work on. I find scrapbooks are useful as the pages are large enough that your notes at the top can be expanded below when your therapist asks you questions.

Remember to write the date each time you open your book, eg. when a memory fragment pops into your head, get it out by writing or drawing it. Then you can get on with your day.

CONTENTS

Foreword
About the Author
Author's Note

Part 1: To Change or Not? (Victim Mode)

Chapter 1	Readiness to Change	Page 1

Part 2: The Healing Journey Begins (Survivor Mode)

Chapter 2	Boundaries and Attachments	Page 18
Chapter 3	Relationships and Attachment Styles	Page 33
Chapter 4	Trust and BRAVVING	Page 46
Chapter 5	Core Needs, Beliefs, Values and Schemas	Page 53
Chapter 6	Betrayal and Betrayal Blindness	Page 68
Chapter 7	Coping with Overwhelming Feelings	Page 76

Part 3: Claiming the Present (Thriver Strategies)

Chapter 8	Validation	Page 93
Chapter 9	Nurturing	Page 101
Chapter 10	Building Resilience	Page 123
Chapter 11	Appendices	Page 147

References	Page 161
Resources	Page 162
Acknowledgements	Page 165
From the Publisher	Page 166

PART 1:
To Change or Not? (Victim Mode)

READINESS TO CHANGE

Human Declaration #1:
"I am me. I am unique. I am different from everyone else. I have the inalienable right to be myself. I have the right to decide my values and lifestyle. The right to act in ways that promote my dignity and self-respect. My life is no longer to be determined by my past, self-defeating beliefs, or, by what people may think of me. Just do what's right, do the best you can and treat others as you would like to be treated."

This handbook is written to help those people out there who want to move past their present situation of nightmares, body feelings, and flashbacks that are becoming harder and harder to sit with.

Situations like this can arise out of:
- Domestic violence and abuse from a very young age.
- Emergency Services workers.
- Accidents such as car crashes, bushfires, droughts, floods.
- Being a soldier or caught in war zones
- Abuses from institutional situations such as workplaces, schools, churches, doctors, Defence, and therapists.
- Trauma from increasingly common droughts due to global warming.
- COVID-19 and mutations have made it difficult to connect with family interstate and overseas and have resulted in often long-lasting symptoms.
- Stolen generations and the deliberate isolation of First Peoples away from their traditional Country/places to destroy their cultures and languages. This is the tip of the iceberg. Underneath are Indigenous people who have been hidden inside colonial families for safety. Then this becomes a family secret so that the government doesn't know. My family is one of those. It makes knowing who you are a challenging prospect.

Many families are dysfunctional and are often intergenerational, as indicated in some of the above examples, and little children usually bear the brunt of significant others' rage and other emotional, physical, and sexual abuses out of an inability to cope with the inner demons that they struggle to carry.

South Australian figures (2010) are that 1:3 of women and 1:6 of men are survivors of childhood sexual abuse. However, there is still a shortage of trauma-informed mental health psychiatrists and psychologists in Australia, especially in regional areas. In capital cities, the good ones have closed books because clients with trauma histories can take years to unlock. Having lived with and experienced all these disturbing facts, I decided to write this handbook. Survivors are helping other survivors.

Middleton (2005) cites Mollon (2002): In abusing a child, "...a significant part of the motivation of the abuser may be to evoke protectively in the child the unwanted negative images of the self – to make the abused one feel utterly helpless, humiliated, shamed, violated and abject – and to bring about a near annihilation of the true self of the abused."

This means that you can feel like an object that is extremely interesting to abusers.

Further, Middleton (2005) notes: "Destroy the cultural and spiritual heritage, sense of belonging, role models, and sources of self-esteem for an individual or an entire cultural group, and the consequences are similar, singly or collectively. Entire indigenous peoples have been eradicated, and in Australia, this total annihilation almost succeeded."

I spoke with a war veteran recently. He said, "No one knows how horrible war is. It is very dreadful, horrible, shocking, and appalling." Wars are also dehumanising because you are given a number and then end up becoming entangled with your troop. You come out of it with a reduced sense of self and a new feeling that home is unreal/surreal and often hard to understand and heal from.

Now, we can see the depth and breadth of abuse in our society and the world. It includes abuse of Planet Earth. We are even leaving rubbish on the Moon and Mars. It speaks of a kind of aloofness, selfishness, and lack of care that has pervaded our species in its adolescence (Homo sapiens hasn't matured yet).

Now, let's get down to business:
Trauma memories come when the brain thinks the person is ready for the information.
Time is irrelevant – **slower is faster** (TDU motto) -- take baby steps.

Think about what you are interested in changing or what changes you may have to cope with that are neither your decision nor your choice to make and which making changes for your health and safety are virtually impossible. For example, when I first started with a psychologist in regional Australia, I was in an abusive relationship, so I used to hide my diaries and workbooks in a safe place. It's tough to change from any situation you may encounter. Do what you can with what you have.

There are always costs and benefits associated with change, which are linked to both our perception of change and our ability to manage it. If you lack the skills needed to enable change and have someone in your community to support you, read on. This handbook contains many skills.

Take from this handbook what you need, then keep it as a resource book, hand it on, or hand it on to, e.g., the Community Centre or medical centre, so that it may be used to help someone else.

An Overview of Trauma and Complex Trauma

My impressions of Trauma: "Trauma is like lightning hitting a tree. It shakes the tree's foundations to the core. It can kill or maim the tree, making it susceptible to attack from microorganisms like bacteria, fungi and mistletoe. If it survives and conditions improve, the tree may be able to fight off the attacks. If it's mistletoe, it can drop the branch or... become overwhelmed by the mistletoe. It's a tricky place to recover from Trauma. Boundary development is also affected: no safety and no control. Trauma is an intensely painful emotional experience rather than a character pattern. It can easily lead to compliance and learned helplessness."

Far too commonly, Trauma starts very early in a child's life.

Suppose extreme Trauma occurs before the age of about four. In that case, one's ego development is altered such that a solid sense of self flies out the window because the brain, always intent on self-preservation, forms another personality to take the abuse. At the same time, the host person remains blissfully unaware. This is the gift that the brain gives to the host personality. Meanwhile, the child is likely to live in an abusive family if this starts at age two; for instance, then further abuses cause the brain to develop yet another personality to take further abuse.

The upshot is that the host doesn't know that other personalities/alters will never tell the host about the abuses. Trauma disrupts the stress-hormone system so that people cannot integrate traumatic memories into conscious mental frameworks without expert help.

This means the host generally sees and feels nothing but moves through life feeling confused: "Who am I?" having weird dreams, nightmares, and sometimes highly charged flashbacks. Sometimes, soldiers who go to war get triggered by what's happening and then retriggered by childhood traumas. We met them at Belmont Private Hospital, Brisbane. The amygdala is highly developed in the **brain's right hemisphere** as it is the keeper of emotional states and autonomic arousal. It knows nothing about reasoning or cognitive functions.

Meanwhile, the left frontal cortex is shut down, particularly Brocca's area—the centre for speech. Thus, the **left** side of the brain does the thinking, while the **right** side has the pictures.

An example of this from my life is that I used to have recurring dreams that made no sense. Sometimes they would change slightly, but often not. After one of these dreams, I would wake up in panic without immediately knowing where I was. The past and the present get muddled up.

Also, the hippocampus shrinks as more traumas occur. The frontal cortex acts as the supervisory system for integrating emotional and cognitive functions, but it shuts down in a panic attack, meaning that we lose our voice and can't move—we freeze.

Trauma creates chaos in the brain. The amygdala creates hypervigilance or hypervigilance. Trauma freezes thinking. It's now fight/flight/freeze/fawn. Research shows that FREEZE is the most common reaction.

When an individual has suffered repeated abuses over the formative years, and it has started very young, the brain has become accustomed to forming new personalities. The person has a dissociative nature of self, not feeling the body - feeling numb, shut down, blank, and frozen. Meanwhile, the person can experience physical ailments such as chronic constipation, and threats can feel real even if they are not. The world can feel intensely unsafe.

The body remembers - EVERYTHING.

The Dissociative Experiences Scale is included at the end of this handbook. I have also included a checklist for how to find a good therapist: What to look for, professional boundaries, and who can help you as a third party, like a social worker, who can go with you to check out a therapist. A social worker will also be helpful for your first NDIS interview. This can be stressful at first, so having someone else there can be like an ally with another set of eyes and ears. If you two can think of questions to ask the assessor, the social worker can ask the questions for you. It is about having an advocate with you. Then you can discuss what happened afterwards. By the way, when you go for that first interview, you must be mentally on your worst day. The first impressions are the ones that stick with NDIS.

One more thing: The public health system does not cover mental health well at all, so if you can avoid it, steer clear of mental health lockups in general hospitals. We had to go into a mental health lockup in Victoria, and it was worse than being in prison, at a guess. That experience stopped our suicidal ideations and attempts! Furthermore, once you have a mental health label on their files, if you go in for a physical ailment, you can be automatically treated as a crazy, psychotic person and be given a red tag on your file. That cannot be very comforting, as we found out in Brisbane. We were completely ignored for five hours until my son thought to ring my phone at midnight. He was in Melbourne, but even so, he got me a bed and a doctor. I had no power and did not know how to call a nurse, so he saved me. This may sound familiar to you, unfortunately. So, it would help if you had an ally, like a social worker, doctor, or counsellor, to back you up. I understand that now, so I am happy to pass this information on to you.

Preparing for the Journey of Self-Discovery

The tools in this handbook address a range of reactions and lack of skills that survivors experience.

In so saying, change from not knowing to knowing depends on our expectations of change. One of the main reasons that change can be challenging is that we are still determining what the brain will show us. This makes us feel that we are spiralling out of control, so it helps to find someone, ideally trauma-informed but otherwise a health professional you can trust (Chapter 3), with whom you can do your trauma work. This trusted other does more than be present when a new memory arises. These people provide **validation** – an enormously powerful word that says: 'someone believes me!' Also, this trusted other needs to be therapeutically confidential in their behaviour.

We can ask this person how they work. It is your right to know. Information on Finding a Counsellor is in the Appendix.

It also helps to have a safe place to go to, especially when we feel unsafe with the new information about our past (Oksana, 2001). In our past, we were not safe, so memories from this time can bring up feelings of danger, threats, anxiety, fear, and the desperate need to HIDE.

This **safe place** can be actual, such as our car, a bush/beach walk, a work/garden shed, or metaphorically, a safe place inside our heart centre or a cloud that floats behind us that can contain a scary memory. Use your imagination. It needs to be something that resonates with you. We tried lots of things before settling on a little, carefully decorated box to put things in to take to therapy. Since then, we have used an A4 envelope. These containers work because the memory information is not lost; it is contained safely to work on with our trusted others. This sort of container keeps our daily life separate from the memory work. This is important, especially as we need to live in the present time with family, friends, work, etc.

I am not saying this is easy, especially when we come from a chaotic lifestyle in which there are repeated abuses, conflicts of trust vs. mistrust because we learned to switch off trust as children in order to survive, and thoughts that we are inherently flawed—that it is all our fault. We have been shockingly betrayed, and this hurts. **Betrayal** is an act, not an emotional feeling. See Chapter 6.

Change is inevitable; however, given recent events like COVID-19, mouse plagues, bushfires, and flood clean-ups, we feel part of a group of other people, all coping with these things rather than feeling alone.

When the weight of flashbacks and nightmares gets too great, such that it interferes with daily life, then it is time to find help.

If you have or can get private health coverage, get top hospital coverage and contact Belmont Private Hospital in Brisbane. Get a cover that gives you unlimited hospital admissions.

In country towns, therapists are there but often do not announce their presence due to the way families can downplay one's need for help. However, your GP will know if there is someone in town or in an adjacent town. Some of them do outreach, and some do FaceTime now. This means that you can have a session in your car when you 'go shopping,' say.

When we start therapy, it can go something like the Kübler-Ross change curve (Change et al., 2019), from initial **shock** to steadfast **denial**, then **frustration** that things feel different now, then to **depression** because "Oh, it must be true!", to **experimentation** with the new situation, then up to **decision** where we start to settle into the new awareness of self, and finally to **integration** in which we are thankful that the part who told us the trauma saved our young life.

It does not matter where or what kinds of trauma we have experienced. Be it a domestic, institutional, natural disaster, workplace, war-induced, or accident; trauma can knock us off the place we were in, in all senses of the word "place". It may be self-image, safety, physical, environmental, spiritual, home, neighbourhood, and mental stability.

Add more examples from your own experiences of 'place' here:

Traumatisation can involve abandonment, either in childhood with chronic losses of care or later when organisations or governments do not validate trauma-related shocks. This then can develop a feeling of **toxic shame**: "You are not important. You are not of value." This is incredibly painful, but not until it is pointed out to you will you realise where the pain belongs. The world feels unsafe, and emotions feel dangerous, so we hide them and feel nothing except numbness. Sometimes, anger can flash out, which can be appropriate or inappropriate.

It does not matter. Only the shock it gives us matters because it indicates deeper issues, we are unaware of.

Abandonment leads to distorted, confused, or undefined boundaries, especially when significant others abuse the child repeatedly, allowing no clear boundaries around the child. This is when children can blame themselves for the abuses and feel ashamed of their inadequacy. **Self-blame** is a survival mechanism because it allows us to keep living in an abusive environment that also gives us a roof over our heads and food. At the same time, children can feel deeply ashamed of themselves. This, over time, becomes a toxic shame that invades our school years and other groups we may join as we grow up. Once grown, we still carry Toxic Shame. It colours everything we do.

Once we realise that it was not our fault, we are faced with issues around betrayal, blindness, grief, anger, body pain and tension, distress, loss of childhood, and lack of sense of self. We want to avoid these painful emotions we try to suppress until we have someone safe to help us through the black hole to the other side of knowing and clarity. Once we start working with this safe person, we have to verbalise the above issues for the first time. This can be not very comforting because we might have been told to tell no one, to keep it a secret, or else. We are also faced with suppressed emotions.

To help us work with our emotions, here is a feedback loop of sensations, thoughts, core beliefs, feelings, and behaviours:

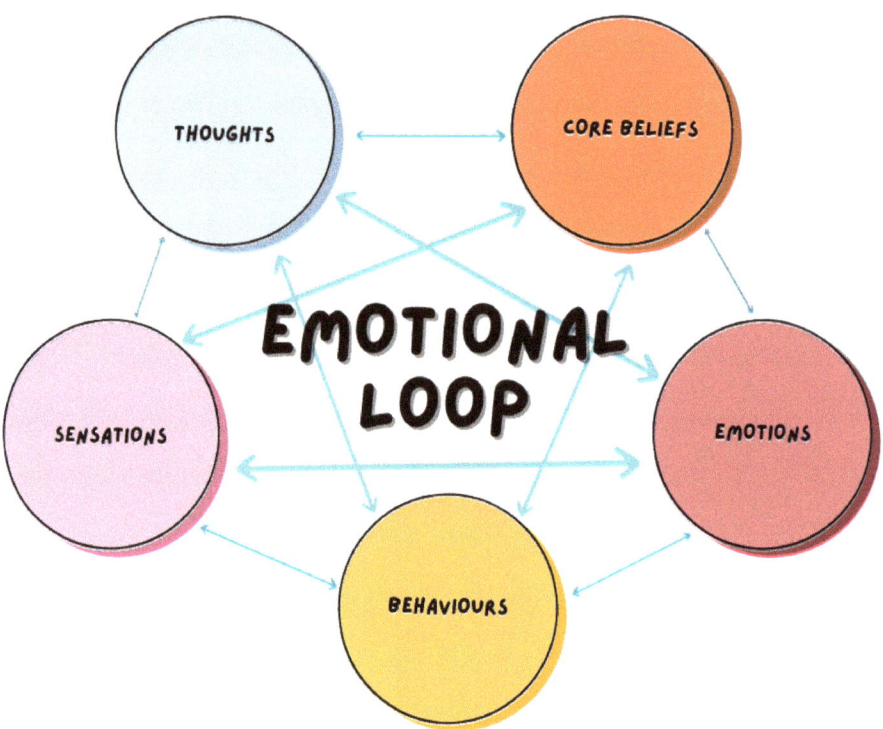

They are all interrelated, and each circle can emerge first, such as sensations. Then, this can jump to core beliefs.

So, the way to tackle this work is to **STOP**!

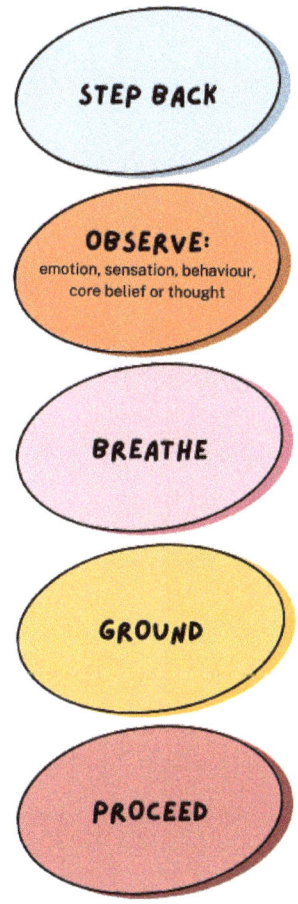

Be MINDFUL that this emotion or thought is benign. They occur and, therefore, can be observed as outside of us. They give us information.

Another more sinister aspect of trauma is **grief**. This takes ages to work through and can pop up anytime. I used to burst into tears for no apparent reason, then find it was grief when I looked at a Mum and child in the street and saw a connection between them that I had never had. This can be very distressing.

Anger involves things we have no control over, e.g., coercion and manipulation, rage and violence, abandonment, punishment; it is my fault and fear. Anger takes a long time to resolve into assertiveness. Anger is on a continuum from **rage** at one end to **depression and suicidal ideations** at the other end. Many abuse survivors sit at the depressed end of things because ANGER is a scary thing to deal with, and it can feel as though you are taking on the anger of the abusers. Sometimes, we can turn on others with angry outbursts. Our anger was in FREEZE. We had no power to change things back then; it was a matter of survival, so we froze. For example, a small child cannot outrun an adult. It is the reptilian response to any attack – a lizard will lie tummy up in your hand, and a dog will roll over to expose his/her tummy, too. This is the RED zone of 'polyvagal theory' (look this up).

Sometimes, after getting trauma memories out and thanking each part for saving our life, we can go from shock to experimentation quite quickly. Then, integration follows. However, try not to think about "time" in this work. It always takes the time it takes. Also, the Trauma and Dissociation Unit at Belmont Private Hospital has a saying: "**Slower is faster.**"

Here are some hints if you are a survivor of childhood abuse:

- Once a new part or memory is up and fitting into your system, you can pre-contemplate the fit, contemplate the part's role, prepare a fit, and then test it out and about. If it doesn't work, we can relapse into Contemplation again. Maybe that part/alter needs a stronger, more important new role?

- A trauma nurse once told me that the parts/alters are enduring, but their roles can change (pers. comm. L. Seager, 2012). Understanding this was a paradigm shift (Kuhn, 1962) in our thinking.

- We started with a map of parts that were usually out and those that were inside, hiding or watching. It has taken some years to work through things like what emotion this part holds, what a part likes to do, or who else it knows in our internal system, like in alliances. Who knows who? This is quite rewarding work. Put an A3 piece of paper on the wall and start filling in information as it occurs. For example, one part may love horses; another part likes other parts and older parts sometimes look out for younger parts. Who are the watchers?

- A clue to finding a trauma event can lie in the parts/alters who are the Watchers:

Who saw it happen?

- Here is an exercise to use along your journey. Find a workbook that suits you, such as a scrapbook or a journal. If you finish one book and then start another, annotate Book I, etc. Also, date your entries.

This takes a little practice, but it helps to know when you record ideas, thoughts, memories, etc. With each question, consider:

The present.

The future.

1. What helps the journey? Who helps?

2. What hinders or obstructs?

3. What distracts me? Where do I get caught up?

4. Are there any challenges that seem fearful?

5. What are the practical steps needed?

6. What are my primary sources of empowerment?

Notes:

PART 2:
The Healing Journey Begins (Survivor Mode)

BOUNDARIES & ATTACHMENTS

Human Declaration #2:
"I have the right to be treated with courtesy and respect – as a capable human being – in ways that recognise my human dignity. I may not always do things in the way that others prefer, however, I am the one who makes decisions for me, and I alone choose what is 'right' at any given time for things that affect my functioning. I have the right to assess the situation and implement actions that I feel will have the most beneficial outcomes."

2 (a) Personal Boundaries

Setting our own personal boundaries is crucial to being treated with courtesy and respect as a capable human being. They include both physical and emotional boundaries.

They rule our choices. For example, "Yes." and "No." are both sentences. They don't need backing up with reasons and/or excuses.

If we've been violated in childhood and never allowed to say "No." or can't say "No." due to 'learned helplessness', then we have no choices. We comply with the demands of others, try to please others first, endure repeated violations often into adulthood, and either aggressively set limits or withdraw from contact. The world and other people can feel unsafe, intrusive, demanding, and/or burdensome.

According to Middleton (2012) "Many individuals are brought up"... "in essentially boundaryless, abusive environments, and these individuals frequently manifest (a) affective instability (with associated self-harming, self-soothing, and suicidal behaviours); (b) dissociation (with amnesias, derealisation, depersonalisation, identity diffusion, and the formation of alternative identity states); and (c) somatisation (an enduring negative self-perception associated with shame and self-hate); while, at the same time, exhibit (d) a strong attachment to an ambivalently idealised perpetrator. Such individuals are prone to be revictimized" ... "Many find it difficult to trust (see Chapter 4) and are prone to believe that sooner or later everyone will turn on them or exploit them."

Poor or lack of personal boundaries, such as the following, are formed in early childhood. They were studied by Mary D. Ainsworth and published in 1964 in Quarterly of Behaviour and Development, Vol 10 (1): 51-58.

Attachment stages begin with the **pre-attachment stage** - birth to three months. This is often where the baby's attachment style develops and, in a dysfunctional family this may present as little to no attachment to significant others. The baby quickly learns that crying doesn't usually bring anyone. The next stage is **indiscriminate attachment** – from around six weeks of age to seven months. This is the time when babies start to develop a feeling of trust that the caregiver will respond to their needs. If the baby's needs are not met, however, he/she will not develop this next stage of attachment.

(http://psychology.about.com/od/loveandattraction/a/attachment01.htm)

Attachment in Adults with a Traumatic Childhood:

(Trauma Model Therapy, 2009)

Preoccupied/Fearful: These people present as VERY NEEDY, HIGH MAINTENANCE, always seeking validation but not being able to have real intimacy nor any emotional intimacy. NEEDINESS is all one-sided and can present as desperately seeking some sort of attachment.

Ambivalent: These people oscillate between drawing others close and pushing them away. They will approach a relationship to seek the attention that they crave and then pull away when the prospect of any real intimacy with another arises. This never-ending dance leads to confusion on both sides of the relationship. Notice that this behaviour reflects a lack of understanding of personal boundaries.

Avoidant: Stay away; I don't need you; remain emotionally aloof and uninvolved, no matter who the other is – partner, aunt, child, friend. Outwardly, these people present as though they don't care about anyone or anything. They do things themselves with no others' help. If another person insists on helping, they dismiss that with a casual shrug of their shoulders and move on/away. This behaviour shows that relationships are greatly feared so personal boundaries are clearly in place at a consistent distance from the person.

Disorganised: Extremely dissociated and fragmented people with Dissociative Identity Disorder (DID) can present either as a socially adept part who enjoys attachments with others; as a terrified child part who is desperate to get away; an argumentative part who finds fault with anything another person does; or a flirty, sexy part who want nothing else except sex. This part/alter may be quite young (child) so sex only makes her/his ROLE stronger. This makes things worse for the whole internal system of the individual with DID. Here I add that this is EXHAUSTING!

Therefore, this type of attachment mix most probably reflects great emotional and somatic (body) damage and an inbuilt/chronic inability to defend against a severely abusive environment with unsafe caregivers.

Research shows that 20-40 percent of the general population has a degree of disorganised attachment, while 80 percent of children who have been abused have a disorganised attachment to their parent/s.

(https://www.psychalive.org/disorganized-attachment/)

These FOUR attachment types present normal responses to an 'abnormal' world. Their 'sharing radar' is turned OFF. Furthermore, their world is based in the RED Zone in the polyvagal system of our brain. As mentioned in Chapter I, p. 10, this is the reptilian zone where we **freeze** when our life is at risk. Women who have been abused, have lost their court cases because they didn't run. This is mentioned in the TED talk below.

(TED talk - Seth Theory: Polyvagal Theory: Safety and Trauma)

It is hard to learn healthy personal boundaries from this standpoint. An example of starting to get in touch with how you are feeling is to think about the last time you were hungry, tired, scared, happy, angry, sad, or lonely. If you are unable to recall this or it was some time ago then you are probably out of touch with your feelings. This lack of mind body connection impacts on our personal boundary settings.

Now think about the attachment styles of your own relationships. What experiences do you feel have influenced your attachment style over the course of your life? Are there some relationships that you tend to gravitate towards? Can you identify the differences between healthy and unhealthy relationships – what are the features of each? The following diagram explains where each attachment style fits with respect to anxiety and avoidance.

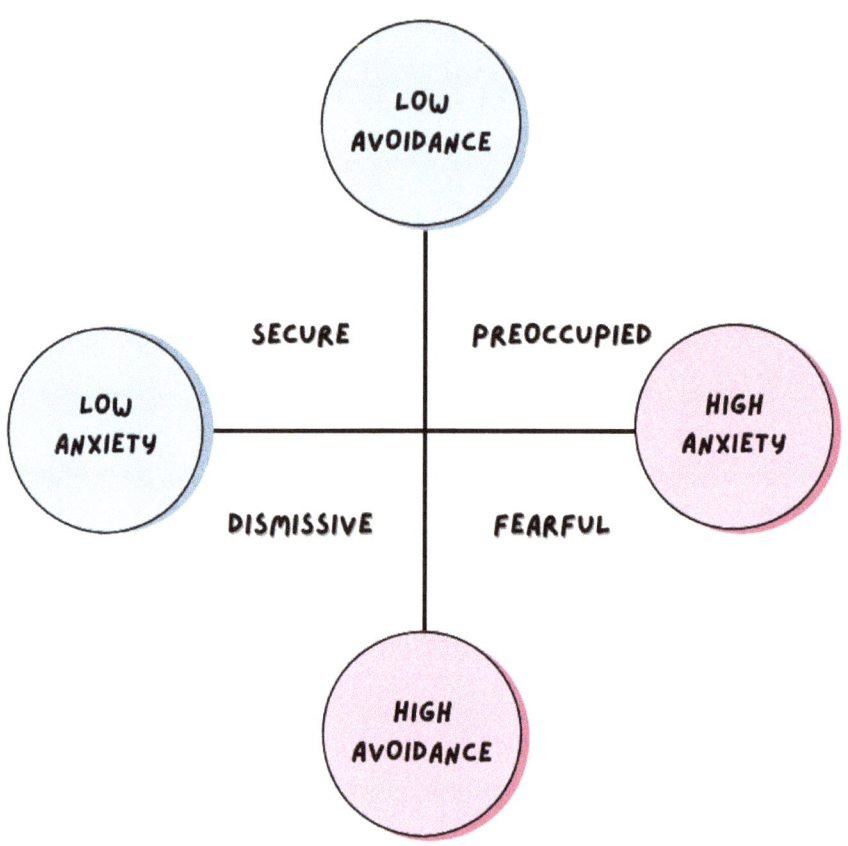

Unhealthy Belief: "I would feel guilty if I did something on my own and left my family or group out of it."
Healthy Boundary Builder: "I have the right and need to do things which are uniquely mine so that I do not become so overly enmeshed with others that I lose my identity."

Unhealthy Belief: "I can never say "No" to others."
Healthy Boundary Builder: "I have the right to say "No" to others if it is an invasion of my space or a violation of my rights."

Add some more examples that represent your own situation here:

The following table gives another perspective on boundaries. Reflect on your experience of these incidents and discuss them with your therapist/doctor.

A Somatic Sense of Boundaries

Boundaries RESPECTED	Boundaries BREACHED
Describe the Incident:	Describe the Incident:
Thoughts:	Thoughts:
Emotions:	Emotions:
5 Senses:	Perception:
Movement:	Movement:
Sensations:	Sensations:

(Ogden & Fisher, 2014)

2 (b) Physical Boundaries

Internally, somatically, our body's feelings and beliefs tell us whether or not we feel comfortable being close to another person. Also, body language is how we sense and communicate boundaries, even if we don't realise it. However, we can feel lost, confused, a target, and hypervigilant without boundaries. We may not have any clear sense of our own values, needs, rights, and desires, nor even our own 'sense of self'. This can manifest as constantly feeling unsafe.

Let's start by taking a closer look at physical boundaries. There are three rules for accurately reading body language (Pease, A. and B. 2007, and reprints). This book is in most libraries.

1. Read gestures in clusters.

2. Look for unity – women tend to rely on non-verbal messages. However, women who are survivors of childhood sexual abuse have lost this ability/radar, so we need to learn it from the basics.

3. Read gestures in the CONTEXT of groups or clusters.

When two people meet and make eye contact, the more submissive person will look away first. So, **not** looking away becomes a subtle way to deliver a challenge or show disagreement when someone gives their point of view. Stand tall, puff your chest out, and look strong.

Practise this. Use the Power Stare: Narrow your eyelids and focus closely on the other person. Don't blink. Move your eyeballs first, and then let your head follow. Keep your shoulders still.

There are eight most common lying gestures:

1. Mouth cover

2. Nose touch

3. Itchy nose

4. Eye rub

5. Ear grab

6. Neck scratch

7. Collar pull

8. Fingers-in-the-mouth – person needs reassurance.

Check these out while watching television and observe politicians at Question Time. If this is not fun, try picking gestures in movies on Netflix, etc.

There are five common types of smiles:

1. Tight-lipped smile – secrets

2. Twisted smile – sarcasm

3. Drop-jaw smile – feigned enjoyment

4. Sideways look-up smile – coy, seductive (e.g., Princess Diana)

5. George W Bush smile – smirk

The further away from the brain a body part is positioned, the less awareness we have of what it is doing. We are almost oblivious to our feet. Hence, feet and legs are essential sources of information about someone else's attitude. For example, jiggling feet is the brain's attempt to escape what is being experienced. Lying increases foot movements.

If the feet are turned away while the head is turned to you and smiling, the person's underlying preference is to escape.

Friends angle their bodies at 45 degrees for open positions, and trouble is face-to-face. For closed positions, intimacy is 0 degrees.

Using these hints, think about a close friend, then an angry person. Think about how you can orientate your body against an angry person. Our body responses are our cues that we need to notice and act on. This is how we can feel safer, rather than the usual submission position of learned helplessness.

2 (c) Touch Boundaries

These are different from the other kinds of boundaries. Whether or not we wish to be touched by someone else and how we perceive the need for touch are pivotal issues around Touch Boundaries. As mentioned above, Touch Boundaries are important for our overall sense of safety and well-being under Personal Boundaries. When we have been traumatised, the vagal nerve at the base of the brain relays the message to the body organs that we are not safe. The Red Zone is where we usually sit.

Think about how far away you wish to place your boundaries. Maybe it's as far out as your arms when stretched out on each side of you. Rotate around this area to see how it feels. How does your body respond to this tangible boundary? Does it need to be further out to give you a somatic (body) sense of more, safer personal space?

Try this: Place your feet slightly apart until you feel a stable base or tree trunk. Now, wave your arms up and out like the branches of a tree. This is usually people's own space. How strong or weak you need this boundary to be is up to you and your home situation, e.g., having young children. Note your thoughts, feelings, and memories. Once you feel comfortable with your boundaries, you have the right to say "No." if anyone/another person encroaches on your boundaries.

Practise this until it becomes a natural awareness of your boundaries; this will naturally lead to respect for the Touch Boundaries of others.

This practice is also GROUNDING. When you are in a safe spot, be a tree and breathe out, then in. Breathing OUT is easier to start with than breathing IN, which just happens. I've found it less threatening than breathing IN first.

When you get more used to breathing, breathe IN chest, then abdomen, then OUT abdomen, then chest. It feels nice. I like to do it when I'm walking with my dog.

Cultural Boundary Differences:

I. **Underbounded:** common in Collective Cultures like Asian countries, where people's boundaries merge with each other's. Individuals are bound to each other and automatically say, "Yes".

2. **Overbounded:** exists in Individualistic Cultures, like Australia, with a guarded, secretive, emotionally distant effect. People automatically say, "No." People can be confused and wary of others.

3. **Pendulum Style:** occurs when people quickly say "Yes" and open up, then feel overwhelmed at saying too much, then withdraw or close; they are afraid, ungrounded, and freeze.

4. **Healthy Boundary Style:** We can state our preferences and stand up for ourselves; say, "No." or refuse requests we do not want to meet; and feel empowered and grounded when saying "Yes" or "No."

Most people in Australia haven't done any Personal Development work, so they can repeat boundary behaviours that they have learnt as children, and this includes not having any boundaries if children are abused and freeze. It is no wonder that boundary issues abound in relationships!

Actions:

Rule of three: Say three things and move on, e.g., "Hi! Lovely day! Catch you later." Think of times you've been able to say "No." and feel comfortable about it. Now think of times you've consented and said "Yes." to please someone else.

In each scenario, what are your non-verbal postures, gestures, expressions, and movements? Who can you remove from your life? For example, who feels toxic: manipulative, abusive, and controlling?

Start Small: Plan to step away from someone who is easiest, like someone you think of as a 'friend' but who is, in fact, very needy. Step away gradually, cope with your feelings of guilt and misgivings, and then step away more often. This can be done by saying or texting that you can't meet as usual next week because something's come up.

Remember: you don't need to apologise for saying "No." Suppose a person gets upset when you say "No." That is their stuff/baggage. You have made a necessary boundary! We leave the other person with their baggage (responsibility). Apologising for saying "No" sends mixed messages.

Once we can confidently say "No.", it is easier to bear when others say "No" to us. Then, it becomes empowering for you!

Boundary setting requires explicit, calm, respectful action in as few words as possible. This keeps us SAFE and builds our SELF-ESTEEM and SELF-RESPECT.

NB. Psychological boundaries are subtle. They involve trusting our gut instincts and listening to our inner thoughts. Never ignore these because they keep us SAFE, especially while we are growing our own Personal Boundaries. For example, if someone reminds you of a past abuser and makes you panic inside, it is okay to step back or walk away while you work through this TRIGGER. Talk about it and write it down with a trusted friend, GP, or therapist. This is a healthy, protective CHOICE. I used to write things down in a diary. Eventually, I had four diaries of notes, all hidden in a safe place at the bottom of my wardrobe. I wasn't safe in my marriage. So, the routine to followed when triggered was:

STOP.

Take a step back. BREATHE OUT through your mouth. Then the body will breathe IN. Do this through your nose.

Observe inside yourself and the outside environment.

Proceed MINDFULLY.

Do things that help you feel good. Find a safe place to go to when needed. This can be your car – go for a drive, a garden, the beach, the bush. Listen to the White Noise in your head. Make self-care a priority. I permit you to put yourself first. Honouring both feelings and needs is critical wherever you are. If this is impossible sometimes, spend time later connecting with your feelings and needs to reflect on how much your feelings and needs are or are not met.

Seek Support: Talk with your GP about any ongoing issues and ask her/him about PRNs—these are supportive medications that you can take as needed to calm yourself—and about any therapists in your wider area. Some, like dentists, do outreach in small towns.

Think about your potential supports and add them to the Resources at the end of this handbook.

This chapter will be presented in several parts, starting with the importance of our relationship with ourselves (internal) and external relationships. Then, we will look at attachment styles that develop after birth and how these present in adults, then how our attachment style impacts our relationships with others and our interpersonal effectiveness. Next, we will examine 'attachment to the perpetrator' and how abandonment is created. Lastly, you can use a few tools to untangle your relationship issues.

RELATIONSHIPS & ATTACHMENT STYLES

Human Declaration #3:
"Like all other people, my time and energy have limits. I, therefore, must set reasonable limits and priorities – so that in order to help others I must have the same care for myself as I do for others. My needs have no less value than others."

The Importance of Relationships

As human beings, we are social creatures who need others to thrive. We first learn from our caregivers as babies; then we widen that circle of influences as we start playgroups and then school. We make connections with our peers and other family members and learn about the world around us. As this widens, we learn about our home street, suburb, and our bigger home, Planet Earth, and other planets and moons in our Solar System.

If all this goes ahead in a healthy way, we also start to know who we are: our 'sense of self' and ego, which develop around the age of four. We start with a secure childhood that evolves into a secure adult.

However, if we are born into a dysfunctional family in which our caregivers also abuse us, this healthy development doesn't happen. We don't develop a 'sense of self' nor much understanding of who around us is safe and who isn't. We can feel safer hiding from others and leading a somewhat isolated childhood. This is essentially **survival behaviour.**

In this scenario, children don't realise that they have, deep inside them, values that dictate what is and is not important to them. This is our **nature**, overprinted by abusive **nurture**.

Here is a list of ten benefits of maintaining good relationships. I've spaced them out to help you improve on each one. Use a pencil as this allows for changes. You may like to document your behaviour in each, as they occur over time. Date each entry as this gives you information on how you have changed over time:

1. **Trust:** Long-term relationships are based on trust.

2. **Acceptance:** We should be confident that we will be accepted for who we are, regardless of our weaknesses.

3. **Support:** From those people, we can consistently trust over time.

4. **A Kind Ear:** From others who will not judge you. Rather, they give you reflective feedback.

5. **Understanding:** From those you know who get your unconditional respect

6. **Someone to Call on When You Need a Hand:** Someone you trust.

7. **Referrals and References:** The ones who know you and from whom you can guarantee a positive referral or reference.

8. **Share and Celebrate:** This can be with people who genuinely care about you.

9. **Reduced Stress:** It comes from sharing aspects of our lives with trusted, supportive others.

10. **Happiness and Satisfaction:** Equal give and take, and mutual like for one another.

(http://www.expressyourselftosuccess.com/ten-benefits-to-maintaining-good-relationships/)

Attachment Styles

Four recognised Patterns of Attachment are more general than the specific types discussed in Chapter 2. It is essential to revisit attachment styles as they reflect how we are attached to others in our adult lives and how these are grounded in childhood experiences.

(https://www.psychalive.org/what-is-your-attachment-style/)

Secure Attachment: Ideally, from about six months to two years of age, infants form an emotional attachment to an adult who is consistently attuned to them, sensitive and responsive to their needs. If this adult leaves the infant, he/she will become very distressed. When the adult returns, however, all is well again.

Avoidant Attachment: When caregivers are emotionally unavailable, discourage or punish crying, and even push their children away from them, children quickly learn to avoid attachments with others.

Ambivalent/Anxious Attachment: This pattern develops when caregivers are inconsistently attuned to their children. Their children are confused and insecure because they never know what kind of treatment they will receive on any given occasion. Suspicion and clinginess swing back and forth with everyone they meet. Because they cannot discriminate between safe and unsafe adults, they can be very much in danger of re-abuse and feel alone.

This style of attachment is further embedded when children are abused by their caregivers, as follows:

Disorganised Attachment: When a parent or caregiver is abusive to a child, the child experiences the physical and emotional cruelty and frightening behaviour as being life-threatening. Thus, the child is caught in a terrible dilemma: their survival instincts tell her to flee to safety, but safety is the person terrifying them. The attachment figure is the source of the child's distress. Quite often, these children dissociate from themselves. This is the brain's solution to the problem, so the child is not usually aware that this has happened. The child, however, can have memory loss, and gaps develop and build up over time. This includes not only the abuses but also family outings and school times.

Attachments as adults are mirrored in childhood styles. These are:

Secure Personality: Children who have formed secure attachments have secure personalities in adulthood. They have a strong sense of self and tend to form close relationships with others.

Preoccupied Personality: This type is the result of a childhood ambivalent/anxious attachment. Adults are self-critical and insecure. Other adults close to them may view them as 'high maintenance'. These people avoid real intimacy and emotional connections with others. They have great difficulty with trust, and no one is safe.

Fearful Avoidant Personality: These adults are usually highly independent and avoid emotionally close relationships. They swing between feelings that come up when they are back in a childhood abusive situation (reliving it) and detachment from feelings in the present. This type has a worse form:

Disorganised Personality: Extremely dissociated and fragmented, reflecting significant emotional damage and an inability to defend against a severely abusive environment. This is a normal response to an abnormal 'world'.

Sharing radar is turned OFF; the adult is always asking themself, "Who am I?" fearing rejection and abandonment and feeling exhausted most of the time. We can have parts who carry aggression and others who hold learned helplessness. I found this out when an angry part came out when someone took the parking spot I was backing into. Another time, I lost the ability to say "no" and became compliant. After each occasion, I was confused and upset. That was before I found a therapist to work with and start my 'coherent narrative' of past traumas as a timeline.

(Trauma Model Therapy: Colin Ross and Naomi Halpern)

Thus, healing from Disorganised Attachment requires the survivor to form a coherent narrative. In PsychAlive's online course, Drs. Dan Siegel and Lisa Firestone will walk you through this process. Being an online course is excellent because this process takes time: you can return when ready, then leave it for a while. Remember, slower is faster.

(https://www.psychalive.org/disorganized-attachment/)

Attachment to the Perpetrator & Abandonment

Attachment to perpetrators is a form of abandonment because it is primarily the abandonment of self. Over time, it generalises to other things, such as lack of self-care.

Susan Anderson is the Founder of Abandonment Recovery Movement – www.abandonment.net and outerchild.net

These are Susan's 39 features of Post-Traumatic Stress Disorder (PTSD) of Abandonment, as viewed mainly from the adult's perspective:

1. Difficulty forming primary relationships.

2. Intrusive insecurity that interferes with your love life, social life, and goal achievement.

3. A tendency to repeatedly subject yourself to people or experiences that lead to another loss, another rejection, and another trauma.

4. Shame – any feeling of rejection or failure can trigger deeply embedded feelings of shame.

5. Difficulty with trust.

6. The tendency toward self-defeating patterns that sabotage your love, life, goals, or career.

7. Anxiety with authority figures.

8. Heightened memories of traumatic separations and other events.

9. Conversely, partial or complete memory blocks of childhood traumas.

10. Intrusive reawakening of emotional memories stemming from childhood losses – i.e., feelings of helplessness, vulnerability, and dread – without being able to recall the original events.

11. Low self-esteem, low sense of entitlement, and performance anxiety.

12. Feelings of emotional detachment, i.e., numb to current or past losses and disconnections.

13. Conversely, it is difficult to let go of an ex, difficulty letting go of feelings

of rejection, longing, and regret.

14. Difficulty letting go, period (like a dog with a bone) over a conflict with another, as a disappointment, etc.

15. Episodes of self-neglectful or self-destructive behaviour.

16. Difficulty withstanding (and overreacting to) the customary emotional ups and downs within intimate relationships.

17. Reaching impasses – trouble working through conflict with others.

18. Extreme sensitivity to perceived rejections, exclusions, or criticisms.

19. The emotional pendulum swings between fear of engulfment and fear of abandonment. On the one hand, you feel that 'the walls close in' if someone gets too close, and on the other hand, you feel insecure, love-starved—on a precipice of abandonment—when you become unsure of the person's love.

20. Tendency to feel hopelessly hooked on an emotionally unavailable partner.

21. Conversely, there is a tendency to 'get turned off' and 'lose the connection' by involuntarily shutting down romantically and sexually with a partner who is fully willing.

22. Emotional anorexia or emotional bulimia: difficulty feeling the affection and other physical comforts offered by a willing partner, i.e., you 'keep them out' or 'push them away'.

23. Tendency to have emotional hangovers 'The morning after' you have had contact with an ex.

24. Difficulty naming your feelings or sorting through an emotional fog.

25. Abandophobism – a tendency to avoid close relationships altogether to avoid any further risk of abandonment.

26. Conversely, there is a tendency to rush into relationships and clamp on too quickly.

27. Difficulty letting go because you have attached with emotional epoxy, even when you know the person is not good for you.

28. There is an excessive need for control, whether it's the need to control others' behaviour and thoughts or being excessively self-controlled. There is a need to have everything perfect and done your way.

29. Conversely, people tend to create chaos by avoiding responsibility, procrastinating, giving up control over others, making messes, and feeling out of control.

30. A heightened sense of responsibility toward others, rescuing and attending to people's needs, even when they have not voiced them.

31. Tendency to have unrealistic expectations of others and heightened reactivity when they live up to them.

32. Self-judgmental, self-critical: unrealistic expectations toward yourself.

33. People-pleasing – excessive need for acceptance or approval, setting yourself up for a lack of reciprocity within your relationships.

34. Fear responds to people's anger, which unwittingly sets you up to be disrespected by or even 'controlled' by them.

35. Co-dependency is when you give too much of yourself to others, put them first, and feel you don't get enough back.

36. Tendency to act impulsively without being able to put the brakes, even when you are aware of the negative consequences.

37. The tendency toward unpredictable outbursts of anger, sometimes burning bridges to critical social connections.

38. Conversely, there is a tendency to under-react to anger out of fear of breaking the connection or out of an extreme aversion to 'not being liked'.

39. Negative narcissism – preoccupied with self-criticism and worry over how others perceive you.

Any of these issues can emerge in the aftermath of abandonment trauma stemming from childhood and adulthood losses and disconnections. The PTSD of Abandonment is a neuro-psycho-biological condition, a so-called "limbic disorder" or "disease of the amygdala" with symptoms that range from mild to severe. Being left alone is perceived by your mammalian brain as an attack upon your being. It creates an indelible impression in a primitive part of the brain that acts automatically to protect you. It conditions your mammalian brain to react with fear each time you encounter the person it perceives as dangerous to your well-being. Acting beneath your conscious awareness maintains a constant vigil on your abandoner. You experience this as being temporarily obsessed with the person. Your nerves are set to 'go off' if you should unexpectedly bump into them later on or see them with a new love. You are confused into thinking that if the pain can last that long and feel so strong, the person must have been very special. But this is not so. It is just your mammalian brain efficiently trying to warn you not to make the same mistake again. Its earmarks include:

- Intrusive feeling of insecurity – a significant source of self-sabotage in primary relationships and goal-achievement.

- Tendency to compulsively re-enact abandonment scenarios through repetitive patterns, i.e., abandoholism – being attracted to the unavailable.

- Diminished self-esteem, heightened vulnerability, and an easily triggered sense of shame.

Victims tend to have emotional flashbacks, flooding them with feelings ranging from mild anxiety to intense pain in response to triggers that they may not be conscious of. Once abandonment fear is triggered, they can feel momentarily overwhelmed, and some experience "emotional hijacking" – a difficulty reining in one's emotions. If emotional hijacking occurs frequently enough, its chronic emotional excesses can lead to unsparing self-criticism, as well as give rise to secondary conditions such as chronic depression, anxiety, obsessive thinking, isolation, negative narcissism, and addictions.

The impact of attachment style on relationships with others can be huge and life-changing, especially if your internal 'world' is chaotic and argumentative with intrusive dreams and other bodily symptoms. In this case, relationships with others can be very tricky. Different people can pick up on our internal confusion and play us for a fool, re-abuse us, or target us in other ways. This is **revictimisation,** and it is prevalent in traumatised people. So, the more we know ourselves and practice saying "No." the more empowered we become and our self-worth grows. This takes courage and resilience - this is what we bring to the healing process.

Tools

It's important to remember that we are in the process of writing our 'coherent narrative' so we can slip up, make mistakes, or pick an untrustworthy person to talk to. This is ok because mistakes are proof that you are trying. People are always expecting things from us. This never changes. What does change, however, is how we respond to requests. It is healthy to call a raincheck, say that you will get back to the person after checking the diary, or refer the person to someone better able to help them. All these strategies improve our interpersonal effectiveness.

Another handy tool is to keep the different forms of communication handy, like a list on the fridge:

- Behaviours – look behind the behaviour to see what it means.

- Illness/physical symptoms/somatic memories that internally communicate information to you.

- Symptoms with no apparent cause = get them checked with your GP first. If evident, it may be linked with Functional Neurological Disorder (FND). This is common with trauma survivors because the brain is not usually connected to the body: the brain switches off what is happening. I had unconscious falls from childhood that I just accepted until early 2021, when I was diagnosed with FND.

Other people have fits, lose control of their hands and feet, or can't walk because their legs collapse. Look it up. Dr Lehn in Brisbane is the expert on this disorder. He has several Active Rehabilitation Physiotherapists who work in Brisbane. I saw one in Annerley. She gave me specific exercises to do to stop my unconscious falls. I saw other people at the clinic who were in wheelchairs, so I knew their legs were collapsing under them. Look up polyvagal theory. There is a way to reset the vagal nerve that I learnt from a TED talk. Lying still, put your hands behind your head, then turn your eyes to the left and hold for 20 seconds without blinking. Then, turn your eyes to the right and hold for 20 seconds without blinking. That's it! The Vagal nerve is reset.

- Body language: The book is generally available; look up YouTube videos on body language; google Alan and Barbara Pease, the body language experts.

- Social networking

- Verbal

- Touching: passive or aggressive

- Emotional

- Music, poetry, story, art, or gardening. Art is very useful for figuring out our mood. I like to use oil pastels because they are very tactile, especially when I feel angry. Weeding is also very therapeutic.

TRUSTING & BRAVVING 4

Human Declaration #4:
"I have the right to experience feelings, rather than tell myself 'I shouldn't feel...' and then feel guilty because I have these feelings. My feelings are a natural part of my being human. I have the right to express my feelings or deal with them when it may be inappropriate to express them. It is not to my advantage to deny or repress my feelings."

Trust is a sliding door moment in which every moment is an opportunity to connect and build trust or not to connect due to mistrust. These moments are all about communication. This includes the words and body language. Do the words match the body language? For instance, if the other person says, "I never said that.", while at the same time pulling his ear or rubbing his eye, it's a lie. You can't trust someone who lies to your face.

Search: **Brené Brown on BRAVVING.**

She discusses having a marble jar and adding marbles in each small step. Marbles can be removed, too, if a person you have dared to trust for a long time betrays that trust.

Brené Brown describes the anatomy of trust as:

Boundaries: Both parties have clear boundaries that do not get crossed over each other.

Reliability: Say what you are going to do repeatedly, have clear limitations, and do not take on too much.

Accountability: If either party makes a mistake, it is essential to encourage opportunities to be accountable for the mistake, own it, apologise, and make amends. NO accountability means NO TRUST/ TRUST IS LOST.

Vault: Shared information in a relationship MUST be held in confidence. DO NOT share any information that is not yours to share, like in 'common enemy intimacy'.

Validation: We need validation from others, that they believe what we are telling them, and that we feel we are telling the truth if we get validated. This is very important!

Integrity: When we follow our MORALS, VALUES, and healthy CORE BELIEFS. It occurs when we work through the unhealthy CORE BELIEFS that have come from childhood, e.g., "I am nothing/ bad." "I am a pest." "I am unlovable." Sometimes, these beliefs present as voices that speak to us from the past. That's how I became aware of the old core beliefs still colouring my life. Once you can hear the voices and identify who they belong to, e.g., father, write down what the voice is saying and take that to a counsellor or therapist. Once we write them down and speak them out, we have moved them from the LIMBIC SYSTEM to the brain's FRONTAL LOBE. Here, we can dispute what they are saying, thus disempowering them, and the voices gradually fade. It's bliss not to have those voices in my head anymore!

Think about your CORE VALUES — what you feel passionate about, giving you a warm, fuzzy feeling in your heart centre. This might be a love of gardening, care of native animals, foster care, or helping others through poetry or art. These CORE VALUES exist underneath our abusive past as part of our core being, and thus, they can enrich our lives while we are on our healing journey. Doing what we love can also give us a break from our healing work.

Non-judgemental: I can fall apart, struggle each day, and ask for help without being judged by anyone else.

We are undoubtedly good at helping others. Sometimes, helping others occurs to the detriment of our own needs, so this behaviour is a barrier to self-nurturing.

Self-nurturing is not something a trauma survivor necessarily knows about or understands as it usually hasn't been modelled when a child. Often, this is replaced by self-harm. This is very judgemental behaviour because it says, I am no good; I am flawed; or it is just the fallback position when things get confusing, and there is no help.

Also, helping oneself comes loaded with those destructive core beliefs. It is challenging to self-soothe and ask for help without feeling ashamed and guilty. So, we hide our needs underneath the help we give others. Now, we need to be non-judgemental with ourselves because we don't judge others, so why judge ourselves? "Well, it was my fault." No, it wasn't, but it's okay to think about this until you feel ready to change your point of view. Take this slowly – it's challenging work changing this view of self. Also, self-harm can land us in the hospital, where we are not recognised, respected, or treated with care and compassion.

Generosity: Being generous with others means that we can be generous with ourselves. Accept this as one of your values, and it will blossom within your heart.

This may not happen in your family of origin, but it can happen with a friend, pet, child, grandmother, or teacher. Start putting those marbles into the marble jars. This helps to reduce the FEAR around doing anything nice for yourself because there are no terrible consequences now, only healing consequences.

Be careful of PRAISE in a dysfunctional family or with a doctor or therapist: it can disguise GROOMING and feel patronising. If so, LEAVE.

BRAVVING includes genuine VALIDATION from others, without which BRAVVING can be very difficult and even pointless.

Avoid self-sabotage as you work through the above elements of TRUST by choosing a pleasant, neutral, safe workplace. Try setting up where you feel comfortable with your boundaries. This may be by holding your arms and turning in a circle. The tips of your fingers can draw an invisible boundary around you. When you feel this boundary, start walking while keeping your comfortable distance from others. COVID-19 has enabled this process to be quite acceptable these days! For example, if someone near me starts coughing, I automatically step away and cover my nose. COVID hasn't gone away. It has mutated several times and is now classed as 'managed'. It is not!!!

When walking, walk purposefully and look forward and slightly down. We don't look in people's eyes. I used to check all the time, but it's not useful. Sunglasses are a great idea, even when out shopping. These are the new apparel, not the old Trauma glasses we used to wear that distorted our view of the world.

The other tool we can use is to observe others and see if we can detect their boundaries. For instance, if another person walks along holding a bag close to the chest, it may indicate very close personal boundaries. On the other hand, if someone swings a bag freely, that person may be showing rather loose personal boundaries (or may have won the lottery!).

Practising our boundaries and keeping them set allows us to use our voice to say "No." Remember, **"No" is a complete sentence** that is empowering.

(https://www.bustle.com/articles/165346-11-ways-to-tell-if-someone-is-telling-you-the-truth-according-to-science)

By the way, 70 – 80% of communication is body language, especially micro-gestures. Also, truth rarely leads to justice, but that is no reason not to be true to ourselves.

Trusting ourselves and our decisions is more relevant, and this takes practice, practice, practice. We have come from a life in which there was an internal conflict of trust vs mistrust that arose if we had or had to switch off our radar to live with untrustworthy significant others who gave us food and shelter while abusing us. This, then, is a survival strategy. As an adult, though, it becomes a chaotic lifestyle with ambivalent relationships: a normal response to a traumatic past.

Here are some other hints on trust:

Predictability: Trust means being able to predict what other people will do and what situations will occur. If we surround ourselves with people we trust, we can create a safe present and an even better future.

Value-exchange: Trust means exchanging with someone when you do not know entirely about them, their intent, and what they offer you. This is an assumption. With a trauma history, I try to live by the saying: "Assume nothing." I slip up sometimes, and that's just part of the journey. Have it up somewhere visible to you or on your smartphone when you open it.

Delayed Reciprocity: Trust means giving you something now with an expectation that it will be repaid, possibly in some unspecified way at some unspecified time. Sometimes, we can HOPE more than TRUST at first.

Exposed Vulnerabilities: Trust means enabling other people to take advantage of your vulnerabilities but expecting that they will not do this. I do NOT do this unless I am with my trusted psychiatrist. I trust no one else with my vulnerabilities, except my dog. People with a trauma history are not expected to do this.

My self-acceptance is a safe practice of trust. I can put an umbrella up, and under that 'trust' cover, I can put relationship building, an exchange of ideas, feelings, and experiences, reliability, consistency of behaviours, and change. As we move through our healing journey, we can change toward more clarity and a better view of ourselves. It takes all the time it takes under this lovely, colourful umbrella. The other way to use the umbrella is to put the BRAVVING elements on the top and the Vault on the handle. It feels safe.

Also, the friends who stick with you during these changes are the true friends; the ones who leave are not the true friends we thought they were. By the way, when a 'friend' is found to be untrustworthy, you can feel grief and realise that you've been betrayed by that person. It can take some time to get over this shock.

At the end of this handbook is a list of what to look for in a therapist. This revolves around Professional Boundaries that must be in place before you can build a therapeutic relationship with the therapist. When I first went to a therapist, I didn't know what boundaries were, so I didn't ask the right questions or understand what to look for. He was very friendly. This is not professional. Get out! Leave!

Have a think about the professional boundaries that your GP uses, for instance. Ask for a copy of them so you can practise things to look for. Being given a copy of them is also reassuring that the GP has professional boundaries. Some of them don't! This is a brave thing, so take your time and choose when you feel strongest. If this is too hard, ask one of your support persons for help. If someone can get the professional boundaries for you, that's a win.

CORE NEEDS, CORE BELIEFS, CORE VALUES & SCHEMAS

Human Declaration #5:
"I have the right to stop and think before responding to a situation. Unless it is a matter of life and death, I have the right to take time out to consider it rationally and carefully."

Core needs underpin core beliefs. Most therapists won't know or help with recognising our core needs because they are not usually taught in psychology or psychiatry. I heard about them while doing a course called Schemas.

There are 5 Core Needs:

1. Secure attachment to others.

2. Autonomy, competence, and a sense of identity.

3. Freedom to express valid needs and emotions.

4. Spontaneity and play.

5. Realistic limits, such as healthy boundaries and self-control.

Have a think about these. Are there any core needs that you were denied as a child? For example, if a child's early life lacks secure attachments to others that can lead to disconnection and rejection (a Schema Mode), then the child's schemas can include:

- Abandonment/instability (the abandoned child)

- Mistrust/abuse (the abused child)

- Defectiveness/shame (the defective child)

- Emotional deprivation (the deprived child)

- Social isolation/alienation (the lonely child)

These keep the child isolated in their world; they can also make the child fiercely independent, needing no one. Alternatively, if a child's early life was frustrated by unmet emotional or physical needs, this can result in an angry child venting their feelings outwardly. The Schema modes underlying this behaviour can be triggered by:

- Mistreatment – Mistrust/Abuse Schema (people hurt you)

- Abandonment – Abandonment Schema (people let you down)

- Neglect – Emotional Deprivation Schema (people don't care)

- Humiliation – Defectiveness/Shame Schema (people put you down)

These children can be impulsive and undisciplined.

Two maladaptive parent modes result from the maladaptive early childhood modes above. These are:

- The punitive parent (punisher)

- Demanding parent (high standards/expectations).

For example, a demanding parent may force their child to sacrifice their own needs and autonomy to care for the parents or significant others. The child can, therefore, lose all sense of self.

If you are interested in learning more about Schemas, check out thepsychcollective.com. In the meantime, I hope the above discussion gives you some measure of understanding about your childhood.

There's a handy tool we can use to get to the Foundational Core Belief/s. It's the 40 to 5 Method. (See page 105). Grab a pen and paper, put the title at the top, such as: 'What is my foundational core belief?', then write like mad without thinking. The first write will be about 40 words. Then, write it in 20 words. Then, in 10 words. Then, in 5 words. See what you discover. This is how I found my Foundational Core Belief.

That blew me away! Then, you can work with the new knowledge and adjust your lifestyle accordingly. Always try to do this with a supportive counsellor or psychologist, as this person can validate what you have found, and then you can move forward into the emotions that arise with the new knowledge. Sit with the latest knowledge for the time it takes.

"No safe place."	"I am unlovable."
"To survive, I must hide."	"I am worthless."
"Nobody is safe."	"Who am I?"
"I am bad."	"I am nobody."

Core Beliefs involve thoughts, behaviours, and feelings: how we think about a belief, how it makes me/us act, and how it makes me/us feel. For example:

Initially, this is all unconscious, automatic, and out of/our control, that is, until we become aware of each Core Belief. Also, these Core Beliefs are Survival-based, so they are important enough to be respected for their roles in keeping me/us safe as a child. The things the voices tell us are part of our story, so we remember them, even after they have become disempowered.

Cognitive truths grow from our work and include:

"I have the right to feel safe."

"I have the right to my own space."

"I have the right to say No."

These truths align with the Fundamental Human Rights at the head of each chapter.

Don't be too scared of these. Confronting our old core beliefs IS scary! It is enough to recognise that they dictate our thoughts, behaviours, and feelings and then realise they reflect a lack of core needs. Also, remember not to trust others too quickly. Use the body language hints in Chapter 3, and if you'd like more, find the book at the library. I believe there are also online books on micro-gestures.

Therefore, we can slowly and carefully change one old core belief at a time. These have expiry dates that we can choose. Also, once we change our old core beliefs, we are safer and at less risk of re-abuses. I can attest to this.

If you have parts/alters, it can be imperative to change the core belief of the one who is the little 'sex dolly', for instance. Be aware that it takes time, effort, and internal communication to find another role that is as important as being a 'sex dolly', for example. Your inner child/children will tell you about them when they feel safe, and then you will learn about their roles attached to past core beliefs.

Yes, this is scary work, so don't push it. It will happen when the pressure to remain the same becomes too great. Find someone you can trust to voice your issues and validate you.

Validation is the most essential part of healing because someone outside you believes what you tell him/her/them.

Get in touch with your early warning signs, such as distress patterns, intrusive symptoms, or a missing need that results in a mental crash or self-harm. You may only be aware of your early warning signs after the crash. Then, it's a matter of looking back at what happened before you lost control. If you can't remember, that's okay. Try to look back next time. Here, we are looking for behaviour patterns, feelings, or actions.

Talk with your GP about supporting medications for depression/anxiety and PRNs to help you through low points where everything feels too much, overwhelming, or chaotic. We can't do this sort of work on our own. Be brave and ask for help when you feel hopeless.

Lifeline can be a first call because you can trust they can direct you. If not, try **1800Respect - White Ribbon Australia.** This is a 24-hour national sexual assault, family, and domestic violence counselling line for any Australian who has experienced or is at risk of family and domestic violence and sexual assault. It also supports people whose abusive pasts cause them to self-harm or otherwise lose control of who they are. A lot of survivors who I've met find this line very helpful. There's always someone there to listen to your situation.

Carrying the old core beliefs with us through life adds to the burden of Intrusive Symptoms, such as nightmares, flashbacks, loss of time, no voice, and feeling stuck — to name a few.

These can be very debilitating, like having a physical illness. Only this is mental and somatic: we can be in pain too because the body holds the score, and it carries pain in all sorts of places. So, when the GP tells you that all the tests are clear, your pain is most likely somatic.

However, this doesn't mean we can assume it's not severe. Always get the pain checked through your GP. Once you know that the pain doesn't relate to a physical illness, you can believe that it is part of past traumas. Sit with that and see how it feels.

We used to be very OCD (not walking on cracks in the pavement was one behaviour) and had suicidal ideations, isolating and hiding wherever possible. Back pain and stomach pains were chronic. Living in the red zone is awful. Therefore, let's balance that against your underlying core values that are not touched by trauma.

Here is a sample of Core Beliefs and Core Values:

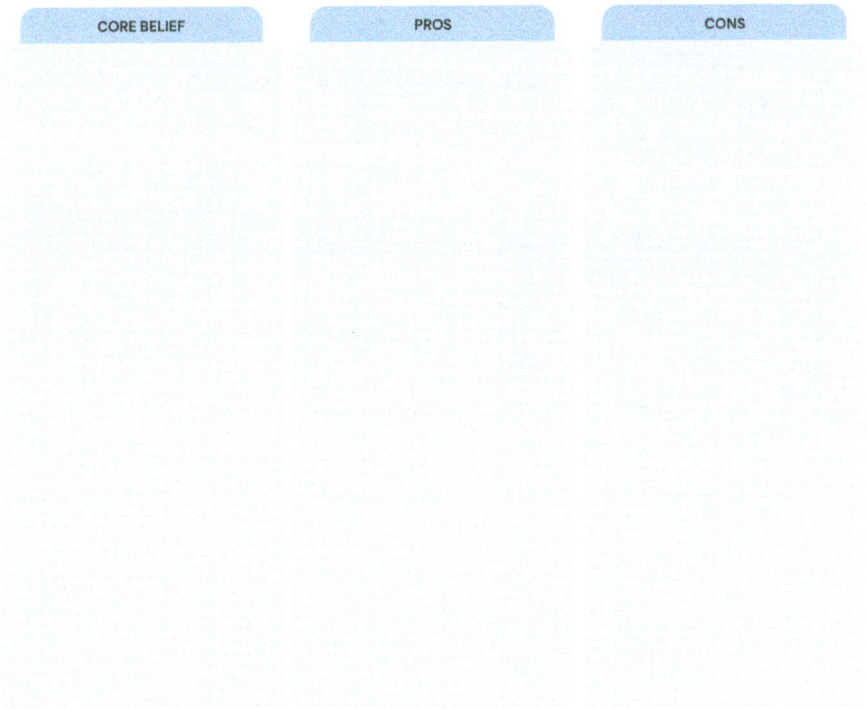

Core beliefs are very convincing — full of persuasion and conviction, so we accept them as accurate without question. They dictate how we see ourselves: worthy, safe, competent, disempowered, a pest, evil, in danger, unlovable, or wrong. Please list your core beliefs as they come to mind, then list the pros and cons of breaking those beliefs that have dictated your life until now. Think of the thoughts, feelings, and behaviours around each core belief.

CORE BELIEF	PROS	CONS

Notice that we have some emotional dysregulation while still feeling optimistic about things we are passionate about.

The aim is twofold: to practise self-acceptance, of being confused and lost, which is believable until we open Pandora's box and peek inside. It is essential to be brave enough to accept yourself at the beginning of your healing journey without judgement and then see your CORE VALUES (nature) that lie underneath your early lack of core needs and learned core beliefs (nurture).

Core values give us insight into who we really are as individuals and what we are passionate about. Our values are separate from any abuses that we have suffered. It's just that being abused from an early age can take precedence, such as having to hide for survival.

This behaviour personifies trauma survivors' tendency to have an Ambiguous/Incongruous range of CORE BELIEFS that are strongly tied to our SAFETY.

Core beliefs or cognitive distortion that can keep us stuck may be:

"I must hide to be safe"

"I am bad," or

"I must do as I'm told."

The first two core beliefs lead to avoidance and reclusiveness in adulthood, and doing as you are told leads to compliance in adult relationships. See p. 26, Disorganised Attachments, Chapter 4.

Once we start listing all these essential core beliefs that kept us safe in childhood, we can decide whether to keep them or change them to healthier beliefs.

Now that we have discussed Core Beliefs, we can look at SCHEMAS. These develop through unmet childhood NEEDS. If we never address unmet Core Needs, they can stay with us into adulthood and keep us vulnerable to attack. Then, under pressure, our coping mechanisms, from the brain's biologically wired, basal, limbic system, are fight, flight, freeze, or fawn. All mammals have these coping mechanisms and use one of them under pressure. For example, my dog and I both freeze when triggered, we are both trauma survivors.

Fight: Over-compensator in the forms of Attention and approval seeker, self-aggrandise, overcontrolled, bullying and attacking, conning and manipulating, or predator.

Flight: Avoidance in the forms of an avoidant protector, detached protector, detached self-soother, detached self-stimulator, or angry protector.

Freeze: There is no conscious/cognitive awareness. This means that when a person freezes, they are highly vulnerable.

Fawn: Compliant surrenderer by being helpful, reasonable, passive, ignoring one's needs, and fearful – "I'm defective."

The INSIDE things, like depression, numbness, and rage, also include Self-harming: our DEFAULT POSITIONS – the things that we do unconsciously. They remain part of our healing journey and decrease in strength as we learn more about ourselves. Self-harming is not your fault. It is a way to have some control in your life that someone else controls. Once you are free of that environment, you can examine self-harming behaviours from the viewpoint of a survivor. Then, you can think about what behaviours can replace your self-harming behaviours. There will be things you can change, such as once you become aware that you self-harm.

While this happens, SURVIVOR'S GUILT can surface:

"I should be grateful."

No! We need to turn that into:

"I am glad I survived so that I can make a difference for others or whatever I am passionate about."

This is our conscious connection to our latent core values.

It is how we grow control of our journey and keep ourselves going. The important thing is not to allow our past to dictate and sabotage our future. So, we challenge our old core beliefs slowly and with support. There is no hurry with this work. It is okay to isolate and avoid when you feel fragile. This is also a way to address a missing core need. The one about setting realistic limits for yourself by isolating and taking time out is now healthy behaviour.

So, a trauma background can make us more assertive, empathic, and proactive once we work through it. It's the epitome of personal development.

A light in the tunnel: With DID, some parts can hold positive experiences, like social parts. Others can be protectors of the secrets. Some are watchers. Oh yes, there are lots of layers of roles. We are allowed to and need to respect the time it takes to find all our parts. Be a curious explorer and thank each part you see, as they all helped in our survival. We need to let go of 'learned compliance' and instead grow our self-esteem by practising saying "No." This can start with saying "No." to yourself, your pet, or plants in the garden, as this will feel safe. Pets and plants don't answer back with retorts!

Cognitive distortions revolve around core beliefs, while **cognitive truths** show who we are underneath it all, as in our core values. Brainstorm this to lower your inner CHAOS and bring clarity to your truths, and then stick this paper to the cupboard or bedroom door so that you can add to it whenever:

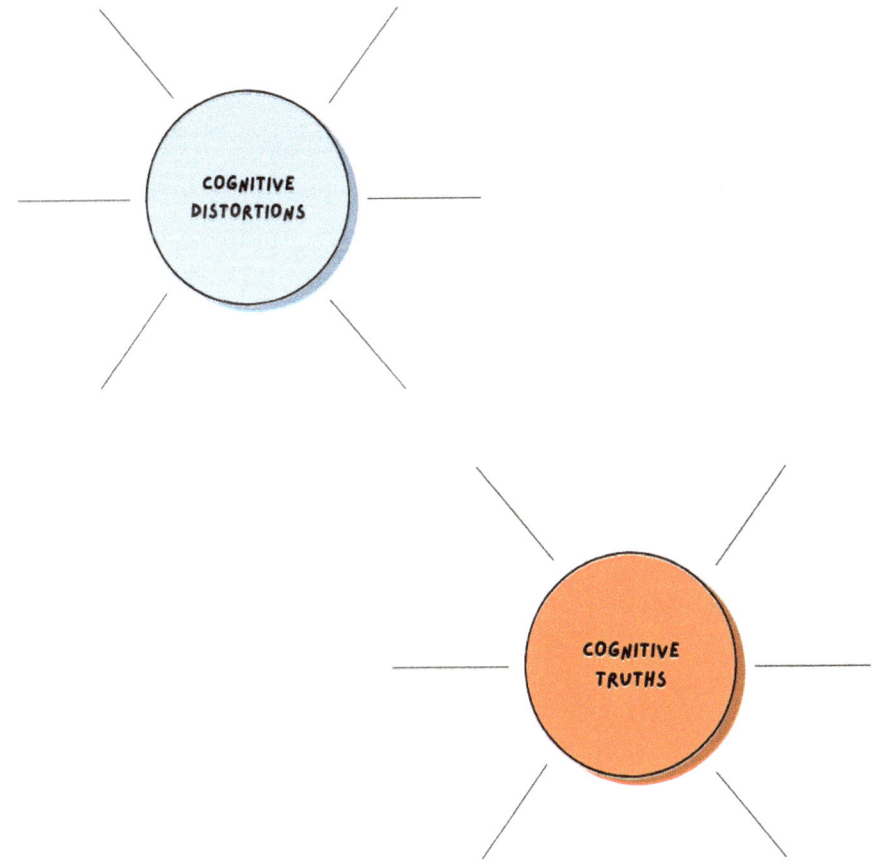

CHAOS revolves around not wanting to speak out our truths [UNSAFE!!] and the confusion around multiple cases of abuse (both childhood and adulthood) and where they fit chronologically. Sometimes, it can feel like your head will explode, and then you can feel resentful. That can lead to anger.

Mahatma Gandhi said:
"Your beliefs become your thoughts. Your thoughts become your words. Your words become your actions. Your actions become your habits. Your habits become your values. Your values become your destiny."

Powerful stuff! He wasn't talking about trauma. He was generally speaking. However, I bet he would agree with the difference between core beliefs and core values.

Look up **www.TheExectutiveCoach.com** for worksheets on how to find your top values, then put them up where you can see them every day. It's fun and a great distraction.

This helps us keep focused on our core values (community-based ones) while we work through our old CORE BELIEFS (what we believe about ourselves) and disempower/change them.

Some examples of VALUES from the list include family, concern (for others), honesty, good will, meaning, personal growth, acceptance, optimism, well-being, passion, support, and understanding.

Using the above: "I seek understanding and well-being through my tough, protracted personal development journey, and I accept that this will take as long as it takes. I will be optimistic about myself and support others."

Practise Radical Acceptance, step by step, SAFELY.

1. Observe that you are questioning or fighting reality.
2. Remind yourself that the unpleasant reality is just as it is and cannot be changed (what happened).
3. Remind yourself that there are causes for the reality: the causal factors of who, when, and where.
4. Practice accepting with the whole self (mind, body, and spirit). Be creative in finding ways to involve yourself. Use accepting self-talk and relaxation, mindfulness of breath, and imagery. Relaxation can be walking and stretching, reading, drawing, etc. My acceptance revolves around: "Don't let the bastards win."
5. Allow body sensations, disappointment, sadness, grief, loss of many things, etc., to arise within you. Write/draw it down, as this moves the stuff from the basal lobe to the frontal lobe. This allows it to become a bit disempowered, and it can be talked about with a trusted person.
6. Acknowledge that life is worth living even when there is pain. Pain is information: sometimes linked with memories; other times, it's part of a functional neurological disorder in which mind and body are disconnected. Find a physiotherapist who can give you exercises to reconnect the mind to the body (refer to the polyvagal theory mentioned in Chapter 3).
7. Do the pros and cons if you find yourself resisting this practice.

Distress tolerance from Dialectal Behaviour Therapy (DBT) (Marra, 2005) can be used to distract yourself. It's a helpful tool that can be used for Distress, Distract, and Vision. For example, VISION is V – seeing good things from my past; I -Imagery of what I want to do in the future; S -relaxation; I – Inspiration (hope, meditation, contemplation); O – one thing at a time to stay on track and focus; N – what small changes can I make to keep my attention on something else. The following is great for distracting away from old Core Beliefs. DISTRACT:

- **Do** something else. Ignore your pain; don't just sit there and notice it. Do something (actively) that does not remind you of your emotional pain.

- **Images.** Imagine something else besides the thing or process that brings you pain.

- **Sense.** Generate sensations that can interrupt your focus on your pain. Suck a lemon, hold ice in your hand, put pepper on your tongue. Chew strongly flavoured gum.

- **Think.** Think about something else. Generate memories, feelings, and thoughts about something different from what causes you emotional pain.

- **Remember.** There have been times when you felt better, stronger, and more capable.

- **Accept.** Accept that pain is a part of life. There is no reason for suffering; sometimes, we must endure it.

- **Create.** Create new meanings. Engage in SPECIFIC PATHS now.

- **Take** the opposite action. Do the opposite of your feelings, even while acknowledging how horrible you feel now.

Giving yourself a regular break from your healing journey is very important. Having this handbook with you means you can put it down and pick it up whenever and wherever. If I had a handbook like this when I had children at home, my life would have been incredibly different, but I had no help. There isn't any/much help in regional Australia. I'm working hard to make this handbook as helpful as possible.

BETRAYAL & BETRAYAL BLINDNESS

Human Declaration #6:
"I have the right to change my mind, to be flexible, where new information or awareness of feelings indicate that it would be logical/appropriate to change a decision. I do not have to be 'right' first time – or even at any time."

Before starting my healing journey, I had never heard of the word 'betrayal'. Then, hearing about 'betrayal blindness' was when the light went on in my brain. Learning about these things that can quietly exist inside people for most or all of their lives is hugely empowering. Now, it's not my business to tell the people in my family who hold 'betrayal blindness', but it helps me to see the patterns and how wide the effects of abuse can reach in a family and community.

Betrayal and grief are at a deeper level than the old core beliefs. Grief pops up again and again. It can hit you in the guts and then end in crying. There it goes again. This is okay. Just remember that we have to go backwards before we can go forward.

As an adult, it is time to look at betrayal blindness. Yes, being abused as a child is a massive betrayal of trust. I also looked at my wider family to see who carries betrayal blindness. Who has betrayed you? Who in your family is carrying betrayal blindness? Who knows what happened?

We can't do anything for those who carry betrayal blindness because this is often a survival mechanism that protects people from the truth. However, it helps to break it down like that and see the big picture.

Try brainstorming betrayal:

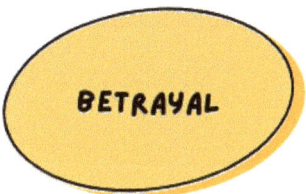

Metallica: And Justice for All: Dyers Eve.

The music is great. Here are the extremely powerful lyrics:

[Verse 1]

Dear mother, dear father
What is this hell you have put me through?
Believer, deceiver
Day in, day out, lived my life through you
Pushed onto me what's wrong or right
Hidden from this thing that they call life.
Dear mother, dear father
Every thought I'd think you'd disapprove
Curator, dictator
Always censoring my every move
Children are seen but are not heard
Tear out everything inspired.

[Refrain]

Innocence, torn from me without your shelter
Barred reality, I'm living blindly

[Verse 2]

Dear mother, dear father
Time has frozen still, what's left to be?
Hear nothing, say nothing
Cannot face the fact I think for me
No guarantee it's life as is

But damn you for not giving me my chance
Dear mother, dear father
You clipped my wings before I learned to fly
Unspoiled, unspoken
I've outgrown that fucking lullaby
Same thing I've always heard from you
Do as I say, Not as I do.

[Refrain]
Innocence, torn from me without your shelter
Barred reality, I'm living blindly
[Guitar solo]

[Bridge]
I'm in hell without you
Cannot cope without you two
Shocked at the world that I see
Innocent victim, please rescue me

[Verse 3]
Dear mother, dear father
Hidden in your world you've made for me
I'm seething, I'm bleeding
Ripping wounds in me that never heal
Undying spite I feel for you
Living out this hell you always knew.

This describes betrayal in terms of the emotions it evokes. At the core of betrayal is loss—of innocence, sense of self, life path, peer group, family connections, and empowerment, for example.

You can add your losses here, or on another piece of paper to keep it safe from other family members or close friends:

Back to basics, BETRAYAL is not an emotion. It is an ACT.

The definition of **betrayal trauma** is that trauma perpetrated by a person or institution on whom the victim must depend. It involves the violation of TRUST within caregiving relationships. Betrayal trauma has specific psychological and cognitive consequences. There are lots of emotions attached to it, such as grief, sadness, anger, heartbreak, vulnerability, stigma, fear of re-abuses, losses, and shame. There is also amnesia for some parts of the abuses. This survival mechanism enables a child to preserve the necessary caregiving relationship. For instance, I'm ashamed to be part of the human race; I'm sad for the planet being used as a rubbish tip. That helps me to manage my betrayals, griefs and losses. I can manage the stages of grief this way: Denial/shock, anger, venting emotions, writing grief letters (without sending them), sadness at the betrayals, and then acceptance of what happened.

It is important to note that, as a child being abused, "betrayal" doesn't come into it. This is because, to survive in the dysfunctional family situation, the child has formed betrayal blindness with conscious or unconscious unawareness of the abuses. Dysfunctional families often contain a lot of people who carry betrayal blindness.

I was shocked when I first realised that I was carrying betrayal blindness, and this brought about a lot of crying. Then, I made a family map of who else was carrying betrayal blindness. That was an eye-opener!

OK. The suppression of memories surrounding betrayal blindness can lead to dissociation – fragmentation of identity, complex PTSD, visual and auditory hallucinations such as hearing what an abuser is telling you to do or what they are telling you who you are, such as:

"You are an object."

"You are bad."

"You are nothing but a girl."

Sometimes, it is safer to say, "It's my fault," especially when you still live in this family who gives you food and a bed. This is a common default position if abused before the age of thirteen.

The way to work through these hallucinatory voices is to write down what they are saying. This is the beginning of disempowering them. Once we have them all down, we can group them under each abuser, then realise that these people know nothing about who I am. This is their way of controlling a helpless child. Now, we can think about who we are inside. This is the flip side of being in an abusive situation, and it gives us our power back.

Note that while you are doing this work, natural feelings of **toxic shame, loss,** and **helpless rage** will arise. Sit with these feelings and allow them to be. I felt loss more than shame: the loss of childhood, of identity (dissociation instead), of healthy role models, and of life path disruption.

You can also feel hypervigilant and/or hypovigilant: either over-observant or under-observant/oblivious of surroundings. Both are exhausting, but they are also essential to be aware of. They are the natural after-effects of a traumatic early life, and they impact and can be re-triggered by adult traumas such as being in a war zone or being an emergency worker.

Betrayal can rock us to our core. Of course, when we look at our dysfunctional family and see how crazy it is, we can feel very alone and isolated, especially when we consider who in the family we can really trust and who is/was a healthy role model.

COPING WITH OVERWHELMING FEELINGS

Human Declaration #6:
"I have needs and have the right to ask for what I want. This right helps me to conserve energy that would otherwise be used up in hinting and expecting others to read my mind. It lowers the possibility of resentment arising from unassertive type requests. I do not 'have to' do everything myself."

Remember that once we start on our healing journey, we already possess a level of wellness.

Let's look at basic emotions and their functions. Learning to read them is quite a skill, especially if you have been through traumas that disrupt this healthy process.

The primary emotions are fear, anger, sadness, joy, and love. Other emotions lie behind the basic ones, such as feeling embarrassed that you feel sad, guilty or afraid. You feel angry, disgusted because you are so weak and fearful, or jealous because you don't have the love of your life that you see in others. You can find lists of emotions online. They can be pretty confusing!

Each person has a range of basic emotions that apply to them. It may be primarily fear and sadness or anger and rage.

Here is a way to connect with your own basic emotions set:

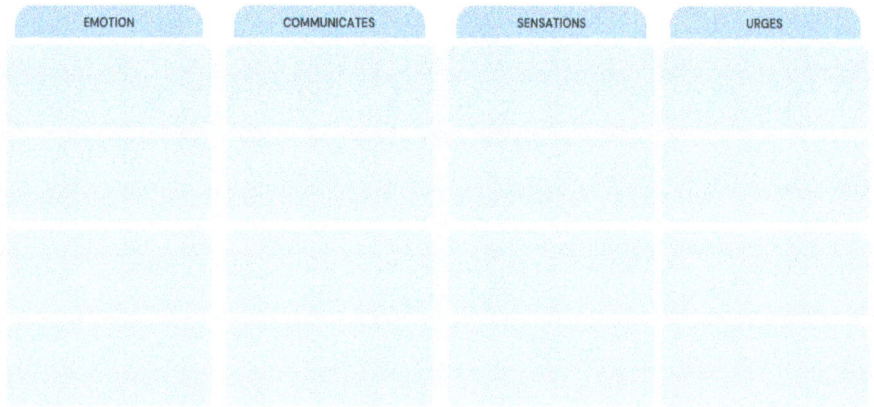

For example, the **emotion** of fear may **communicate** danger through the **sensations** of dry mouth and sweaty hands and the **urge** to escape, which turns into an involuntary freeze.

In this exercise, it's important to focus on the purposes and meaning of an emotion rather than judging it. They are a part of your story and the part of you that you are learning to read, maybe for the first time. Remember to pace yourself. Looking at your emotional patterns is very scary at first and can cause panic. This is normal. Walk away and have a break, drink water, a cup of tea or coffee, and BREATHE.

Let's now look at triggers. These happen anytime, a bit like flashbacks. However, the difference is that triggers come from our surroundings, in the moment, whereas flashbacks come from the past and are more disorienting than triggers.

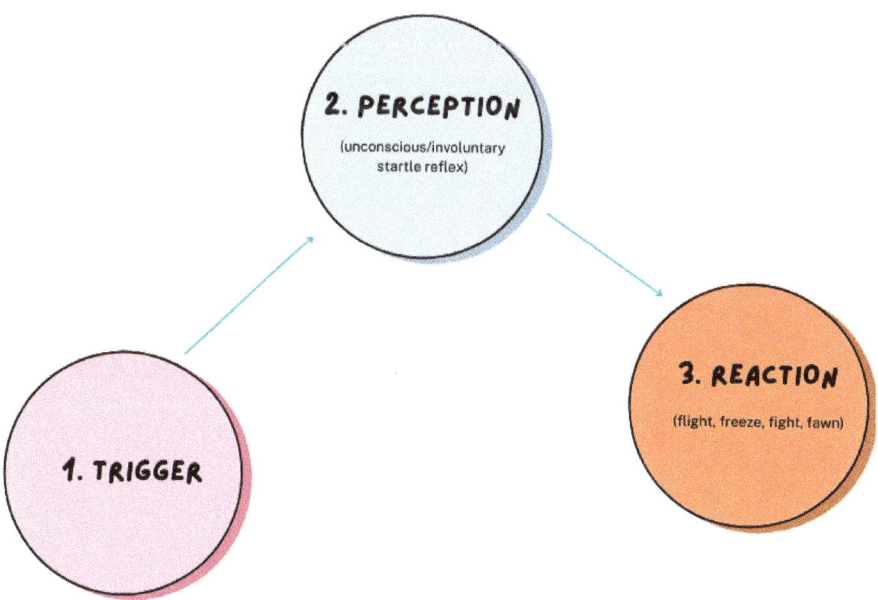

Write down each trigger if and when you are in a position to do that. If you miss one, it will recur. This is how we start to disempower the triggers. Think how you felt when the trigger set you off into a panic attack. Then, consider where the trigger came from in your past. Once you can identify where the trigger came from:

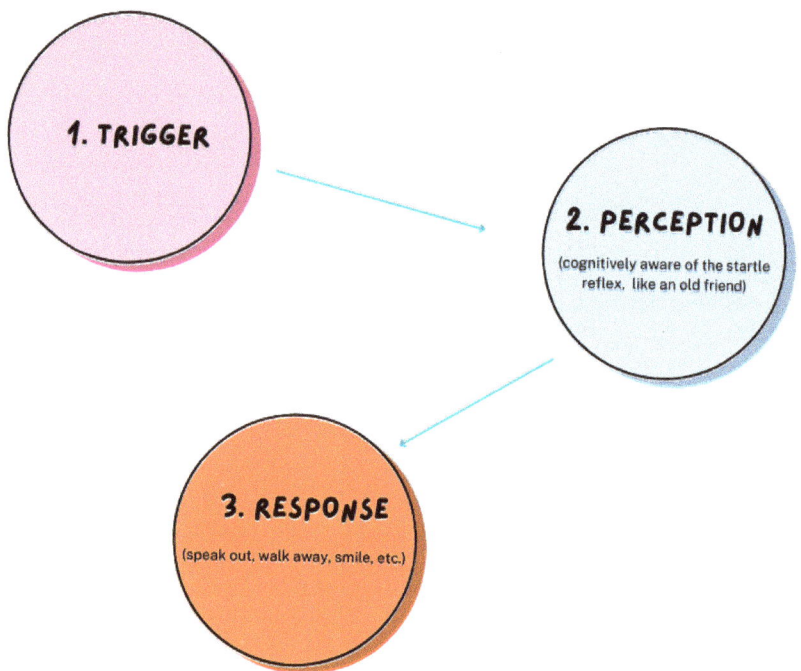

This change in perception of a trigger is called distress tolerance: our ability to withstand emotional distress. Distress tolerance is an important skill to have. Once we understand where one trigger or flashback comes from, such as a person who reminds you of someone else or a smell or sound, by using distress tolerance, the following trigger or flashback that we work on will be easier. Take things slowly, at your own pace, and always use your support person/people to help with this heavy work.

For example, think of a recent time, event, or situation when you experienced low distress tolerance - emotions became overwhelming and challenging to regulate.

How did you behave during the distress?

How could you have better managed the situation to reduce the level of distress felt?

The above questions may seem irrelevant if your level of distress is an entirely natural response to a shocking situation and you understand what happened. Down the track, though, these distresses can help with the ones that occur out of the blue and send us into a downward spiral. Then, our levels of distress tolerance and resilience improve. After we understand, we can think of how we feel and write down the effects of the distress.

Flashbacks are another thing altogether. A flashback can throw you off track and take you to another place and time.

This is involuntary. PANIC!

Here's a way of keeping yourself safe when this happens:

STOP! Ensure you are safe- not in the middle of a road.

BREATHE.

Have a drink of water.

BREATHE. Look around. Reorientate yourself. It can help you return to a wall or tree so nothing can creep up behind you.

Wait until you are present. Take three deep breaths in through your nose, hold them briefly, and then out through your mouth.

Then proceed.

Later, remember to write this flashback down as your record of events. After traumas, parts of our brain keep us on edge: hypervigilant, constantly scanning our surroundings, always expecting danger. Sometimes, though, we can become hypovigilant and do no scanning. It's a bit like learned helplessness, in which we give up and comply. However, there is hope, and we are no longer helpless. We can eventually walk away, say "No," or stand our ground assertively.

Flashbacks are extremely distressing and cannot be underestimated.

If you have had multiple traumas, a trigger or flashback may represent one event and then trigger panic from a different event. Then, a cascade of events can follow. This is exhausting!

In this case, check which parts of your body hold different events. You may feel pain in a spot unrelated to any other physical injury. The body keeps the score—this is also the name of a book. It's true that the body holds many memories of past traumas.

Nightmares

Oh, how these recur over and over again! Sometimes, they change a bit. Once I realised that writing them down helps, I did that in earnest. It helped a lot to see them on paper. Some of them were recorded as pictures of what I could see in my nightmares.

Here are some questions to help you on your way:

Write about your nightmare: are you an observer?

Are there other people there?

Is it night or day?

Are there noises around, etc?

Does it serve a purpose?

Have you used it to gain some understanding of your issues?

How do you currently manage this nightmare?

What works and what doesn't work with it?

Use a mind map:

Then, either sharing them with someone in your support network who you trust or discovering what the nightmare means can lessen the nightmare.

Then, we can target the following string of nightmares with a common theme.

A sleep study on night terrors vs nightmares showed that nightmares tend to occur during the second half of the night when dreaming is most intense during REM sleep. They are "horrific dreams that we recall after awakening, and originate from dream sleep, so dream images are vivid and specific", says Dr Peter Fotinakes, medical director of St. Joseph Hospital's Sleep Disorders Centre, Orange County, California. On the other hand, night terrors are often not remembered on waking because they occur in non-REM dreams and consist of brief, fragmented impressions that are less emotional and less likely to involve visual images. We can be left with a niggling feeling that something happened during the night. Then, it's gone as we get on with the day.

Overwhelming feelings tend to arise when we revisit a traumatic event. For people with PTSD, this experience repeatedly causes thoughts of fear, panic, shock, anger, restlessness, and even horror.

Here is a checklist of questions to help you deal with overwhelming feelings. It can help to get a piece of paper and do a mind dump, as shown below the checklist:

> How do overwhelming feelings currently affect your life?
>
> What do you do to manage these?
>
> What have you discovered that works?
>
> What have you discovered that doesn't work?
>
> Who can you call to help with these overwhelming feelings?

Let me tell you about **THE ANGER STORY.**

Anger is on a long continuum from out-of-control RAGE at one end to deep depression and suicidal ideations at the other end. So, if you usually get depressed, this is how your anger emerges.

Anger can also be viewed as the tip of an iceberg that people can see, like an outburst of anger. However, underneath the water, where the most significant part of the iceberg sits, are the emotions behind the anger that we can't face, such as sadness, loneliness, embarrassment, hurt, grief, anxiety, guilt, jealousy, fear, shame, threatened, stress, frustration, depression, and helplessness. As you can see, these are big emotions, which is why they remain buried.

The repeating cycles are represented here:

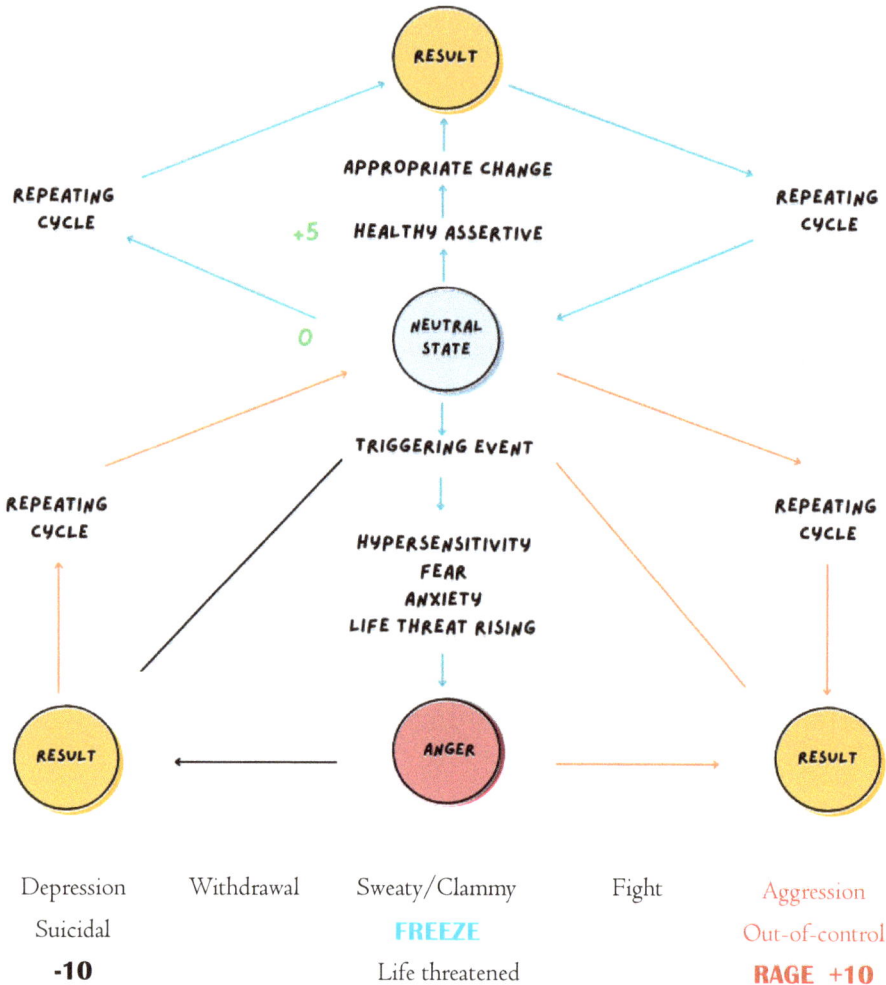

Only when we work through why we react to each triggering event can we change the Repeating Cycle from unhealthy and reactive to healthy and assertive?

Trauma survivors tend to either copy the anger from the violence, punishment, power, coercion, control, silence, or abandonment as rage or depression. This is black-and-white thinking that is very common in survivors. It's not Bad. It just IS.

So now, let's think about the overwhelming feelings you usually feel as part of your reactive patterns that cause ongoing distress.

All distressing occurrences can be portrayed using a 'SUDS' Scale to communicate to yourself and others how much distress you are experiencing and to enable you to apply strategies that will help you to reduce or contain the distress.

SUDS – Subjective Units of Distress Scale

The scale runs from 0 to 10, with 0 being the least distress and 10 being the most distress. Sometimes, it might seem your distress is beyond a 10. If you are at ten or beyond regularly, ring 1800Respect. For example:

0 .... I am completely relaxed with no distress.

1 .... I am alert and awake, concentrating well.

Up to 6 .... My body tension is substantial and unpleasant, although I can still tolerate it and think clearly.

Now a 10 .... Extreme distress.

I am filled with panic, and I have extreme tension throughout my body. This is the worst possible fear and anxiety.

Emptiness (apathy, depression)

"The wounded inner child contaminates adult life with a low-grade chronic depression experienced as emptiness."

(Bradshaw, 1994).

He explains that you are living without your authentic self, so it feels like being on the sidelines, watching life go by.

Emptiness can also be experienced as apathy—having no joy or meaning in one's life. I experienced this as numbness, not feeling anything at all.

Existential boredom can arise out of emptiness and is a chronic state. It differs from situational boredom, which comes and goes, depending on what is happening around you. We may ask, "What's the point?" and question life's meaning and purpose.

Bradshaw (1994) developed a Wounded Child Questionnaire that I will put here to help you understand how a wounded inner child feels and to help you identify if you have a wounded inner child or more than one.

Wounded Child Questionnaire

IDENTITY

1. I experience anxiety and fear whenever I contemplate doing anything new. Yes_____No _____

2. I'm a people pleaser (nice guy/sweetheart) with no identity. Yes _____ No _____

3. I'm a rebel. I feel alive when I'm in conflict. Yes _____No _____

4. I feel something is wrong with me in the deepest places of my secret self. Yes _____No _____

5. I'm a hoarder; I have trouble letting go of anything. Yes _____No _____

6. I feel inadequate as a man/woman. Yes _____No _____

7. I'm confused about my sexual identity. Yes _____No _____

8. I feel guilty when I stand up for myself and would rather give in to others. Yes _____No _____

9. I have trouble starting things. Yes _____No _____

10. I have trouble finishing things. Yes _____No _____

11. I rarely have a thought of my own. Yes _____No _____

12. I continually criticise myself for being inadequate. Yes _____No _____

13. I consider myself a terrible sinner, and I'm afraid I'm going to hell. Yes ___No ___

14. I'm rigid and perfectionistic. Yes _____No _____

15. I feel like I never measure up and never get anything right. Yes _____No _____

16. I feel like I don't know what I want. Yes _____No _____

17. I'm driven to be a super achiever. Yes _____No _____

18. I believe I don't matter except when I'm sexual. I'm afraid I'll be rejected and abandoned if I'm not a good lover. Yes _____No _____

19. My life is empty; I feel depressed a lot of the time. Yes _____No ____

20. I don't know who I am. I'm not sure what my values are or what I think about things. Yes _____No _____

BASIC NEEDS

1. I'm out of touch with my bodily needs. I don't know when I'm tired, hungry, or horny. Yes _____ No _____

2. I don't like being touched. Yes _____ No _____

3. I often have sex when I don't want to. Yes _____ No _____

4. I have had or currently have an eating disorder. Yes _____ No _____

5. I am hung up on oral sex. Yes _____ No _____

6. I rarely know what I feel. Yes _____ No _____

7. I feel ashamed when I get mad. Yes _____ No _____

8. I rarely get mad, but when I do, I rage. Yes _____ No _____

9. I fear other people's anger and will do almost anything to control it. Yes _____ No_____

10. I'm ashamed when I cry. Yes _____ No _____

11. I'm ashamed when I'm scared. Yes _____ No _____

12. I rarely express unpleasant emotions. Yes _____ No _____

13. I'm obsessed with anal sex. Yes _____ No _____

14. I'm obsessed with sado/masochistic sex. Yes _____ No _____

15. I'm ashamed of my bodily functions. Yes _____ No _____

16. I have sleep disorders. Yes _____ No _____

17. I spend an excessive amount of time looking at pornography. Yes _____ No _____

18. I have exhibited myself sexually in a way that violates others. Yes _____ No _____

19. I am sexually attracted to children, and I worry that I might act it out. Yes _____ No _____

20. I believe that food and/or sex is my greatest need. Yes _____ No _____

SOCIAL

1. I distrust everyone, including myself. Yes _____ No _____

2. I have been or am now married to a person with an addiction. Yes _____ No _____

3. I am obsessive and controlling in my relationship. Yes _____ No _____

4. I am an addict. Yes _____ No _____

5. I'm isolated and afraid of people, especially authority figures. Yes _____ No _____

6. I hate being alone and will do almost anything to avoid it. Yes _____ No _____

7. I find myself doing what others expect of me. Yes _____ No _____

8. I avoid conflict at all costs. Yes _____ No _____

9. I rarely say no to another's suggestions and feel that another's suggestion is almost an order to be obeyed. Yes _____ No _____

10. I have an overdeveloped sense of responsibility. It is easier for me to be concerned with another than with myself. Yes _____ No _____

11. I often do not say no directly and refuse to do what others ask in manipulative, indirect, and passive ways. Yes _____ No _____

12. I don't know how to resolve conflicts with others. I either overpower my opponent or completely withdraw from them. Yes _____ No _____

13. I rarely ask for clarification of statements I don't understand. Yes _____ No _____

14. I frequently guess what another's statement means and respond based on my guess. Yes _____ No _____

15. I never felt close to one or both of my parents. Yes _____ No _____

16. I confuse love with pity and tend to love people I can pity. Yes _____ No _____

17. I ridicule myself and others if they make a mistake. Yes _____ No _____

18. I give in easily and conform to the group. Yes _____ No _____

19. I'm fiercely competitive and a poor loser. Yes _____ No _____

20. My most profound fear is the fear of abandonment, and I'll do anything to hold on to a relationship. Yes _____ No _____

If you answered yes to ten or more of these questions, you must do some serious work. This is what John Bradshaw says. His book is available on Booktopia.com.au for $22.50, and the Audiobook is available for $21.39. You can check out the books by googling 'John Bradshaw's Homecoming.'

In the meantime, answering 'yes' to ten or more questions gives insight into your wounded inner child, which can be a helpful starting point for connecting with your inner child/children.

By the way, remember that a wounded inner child is not to blame for how they feel. Understand that it's not their fault to think these ways. However, it is your responsibility to help your wounded inner child/ren heal.

PART 3:
Claiming the Present (Thriver Strategies)

VALIDATION

Human Declaration #8:
"I do not have to be a 'pillar of strength' needing no one else's help or support unless absolutely necessary. I have the right not to push myself to the limit. I have the right to take time for myself, for leisure, for time out, for even being lazy. I can also ask for help when I don't really need it."

Finding people to validate our story is the most important aspect of our healing journey. It helps to not feel like either a crazy person or a liar, and it encourages further healing because someone outside of us believes us. You may have several people who validate aspects of your story. In a dysfunctional family, these external others are often not in the immediate family. They may be your GP, teacher/tutor, friend, or librarian. However, it needs to be someone you trust before you go telling them parts of your traumatic story. You have the right to tell these people that you need the information you ask them to be confidential. If in doubt, don't tell them anything.

A counsellor once gave me a tool to use.

It's called the **Trust Triangle.**

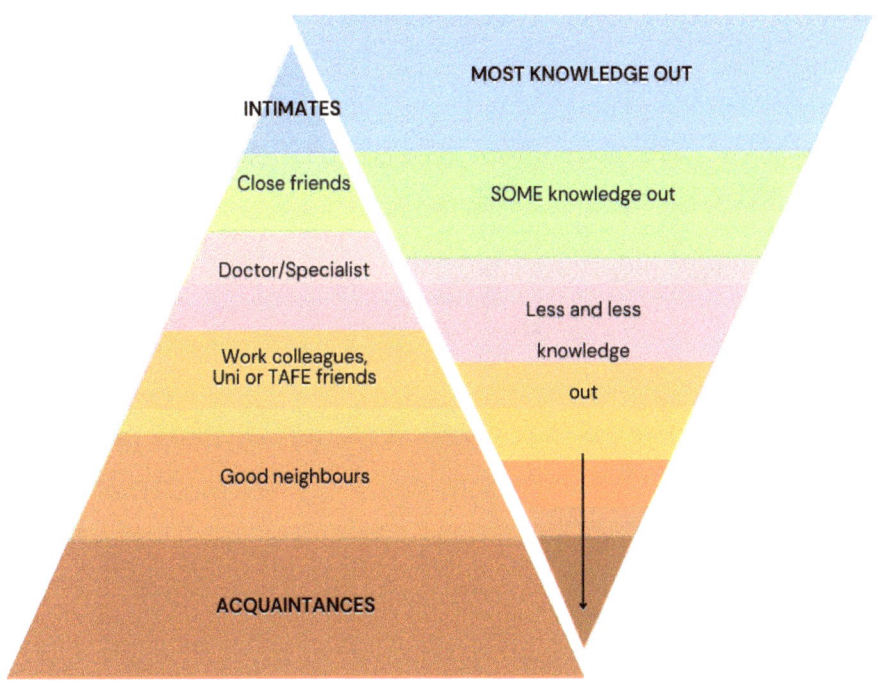

You can change who you tell over time if you see that a close friend is not trustworthy. Friends are for a reason, a season, or life. Some friends I had turned out to be for a season or a reason. 'Oops! I told that person some personal stuff. Oh well, I can't do much about that now.' It's time to move on. It can hurt for a while, though, and can cause self-harming to recur as you beat yourself up.

While you are withdrawn and keeping things private, think of what happened. A thought: I have no right to dump my trauma history onto a close friend. It's my stuff, not theirs. I haven't told my children either because it's my journey, not theirs. They know my life's been rough and complex, but not the details. Or you may think your boundaries dropped with that person, so they could get inside your lack of personal boundaries and cause harm.

However, it would help if you told somebody the details of your discomfort to be validated and worked through the details and made sense of them. This is where it can get hard and why I am writing this handbook. If you find it helpful, take it from me: I validate your story. I know domestic violence is everywhere, and I know how much this impacts your adult life. In the meantime, see if you can find somebody fairly locally to visit regularly and remember to check their professional boundaries (Appendix).

Manifesting your truth as a survivor comes with learning to say "no" to something that doesn't serve you rather than trying to change it or fix it into a "yes." It also comes with acceptance of your truth. Please take this as meaning that trauma survivors have learned to keep the truth of their traumas hidden, not that they don't exist but that the truth is safer being hidden. Acceptance takes time and space, as well as talking around and about the abuses. Once you become aware of a new memory, sit with it, draw it, or write it and see where it fits. This is tough work. A new memory might take a month or more to work through and understand, put it in context and chronological order, and then see that it fits well in your story. That leads to acceptance.

It also includes a shift in your sense of self. The 'who you are' is widened to include the new memory in the present time. Yes, it's from the past, and it can still cause panic, flashbacks, nightmares, grief, and betrayal. But the now is SAFE; the past was UNSAFE. The mind swings from Safe to Unsafe to Safe. This is a normal response to an abnormal early world. Go with this flow, as it will fade into the background eventually. It won't go away, but the aftereffects of trauma will not so severely impact your life once you make sense of the trauma/s and lock it into your life story.

If you don't have any, it can be helpful to ask a family member for old photos of the family and photos of you as a child. These can become snapshot memories of times you don't remember. They can also help with your work on chronological memories.

Processing memories starts with a new memory – ah! How does it present? How do you feel? Write down everything you feel, such as angry, upset, crying out of control, panicky, depressed, embarrassed, feeling exposed or watched, feeling that it can't be true, etc. Feelings keep us alive, so emotions are not connected with memory work. The memory is just that. When you start processing it, your feelings will start firing off. This is validation that the memory is real. You are neither a fraud nor a liar. You are seeing more of your truth in the new memory. That's all!

The rationale of this process is that the logic of the new memory is with the adult thinker, whereas the inner child feels the memory. When you have 'let go' and processed a new memory, you will have arrived at 'conscious coalescence' in which the logical part merges with the emotional part of each memory. This changes how you feel, as you now know more about who you are. This can feel empowering because you have survived your past rather than succumbing to it. This is validation that you are a survivor.

Then, you can shift shame (inner child) to blame (adult thinking) more easily. Trust yourself to do this SAFELY. It wasn't your fault.

An essential aspect of this journey is getting a good sleep each night. I used to process things at night and brainstorm possible solutions. Then I asked a trusted other if she would help. She said 'yes' and wrote:

> "You have permission to stop processing and sleep at night. This is important, and it is part of your healing."

I read this out loud every night for a year until it became a regular thing. I've slept soundly at night ever since. I wake refreshed and can start processing again as I go through each day. Then, before bed each night, write down your thoughts in a diary or scrapbook, plan for the next day, and put the book beside your bed. If you have a nightmare or new memory, write it in your book, then roll over and go back to sleep. You have recorded the content, so it's safe. You don't have to turn the light on to record your nightmare. Have a blank page open with the pencil or pen resting on top. This works well because you can't see what you are writing or drawing and can get back to sleep more easily.

Remember that it takes time to change things, such as difficulty regulating emotions, relationship patterns, losing time, old core beliefs, or feeling used. This work can become frenetic -

"Too much analysis leads to paralysis."

So, slow things down, as there is no rush to finish your healing journey and remember that it takes the time it takes. Everyone's journey is different, and comparing your journey with someone else's can be quite damaging. You can feel sad and ripped off that yours is taking longer than someone else's. Your foundations are unique to you, so building your 'house' at your pace is important.

Do this with self-acceptance and self-compassion. Be gentle with yourself and nurture yourself at least once each day. It can be a coffee out, a good book, a puzzle book, your favourite music, or a walk along the street, park, beach, or bush, wherever you feel that you can breathe and relax works. Hug a tree, plant something, or weed an area. These sorts of activities are therapeutic, too.

While on your healing journey, keep an eye on your relationships: who is important and who can be left behind? As you progress along your journey, you will get better at doing this. If you slip up, that is part of your healing journey – try not to beat yourself up. You are changing old behaviour patterns into new ones. These take the time they take, one at a time. Also, treat others as you would like to be treated. This is all you can do. People often don't live up to our expectations, so I've learned to relax and let people be. Then, I can let myself be.

Another useful self-validating tool you can use is the **Window of Tolerance.**

HYPERAROUSAL

Anxious, angry, out of control

Overwhelmed: feeling too much.

Your body wants to fight or run away. Panic!

It's not something you choose - these reactions just take over.

WINDOW OF TOLERANCE

When stress and trauma shrink your Window of Tolerance, it doesn't take much to throw you off balance.	When you are here, you feel able to deal with whatever is happening in your life. You might feel stress or pressure, but it doesn't bother you too much. This is the ideal place to be.

HYPOAROUSAL

Spacy, zoned out, numb, frozen: feeling too little.

Your body wants to shut down.

It's not something you choose to do – these reactions just take over.

Working with a practitioner can help expand your 'Window of Tolerance' so that you are more able to cope with challenges. I have used this and changed it over time as I worked through my stuff with a trusted practitioner who kept validating my story as it came out in words and pictures in my scrapbooks. I have my latest chart up on the fridge. Decorate your chart with things and pictures that are meaningful to you. Magazines have nice pictures you can cut out, and stickers are fun to use.

Brainstorm some ideas here:

NURTURING

Human Declaration #9:
"I have the right to ask for information – to get a second opinion, to say "I don't understand", to ask pointed questions, to know exactly what to expect from professional services – everything I need in order to make a decision. I do not have to undertake anything unless I feel comfortable that I know what is required. I choose not to allow people (or myself) to pressure me. If unsure, ASK for clarification."

Breathing

Breathing reduces stress in the body, including chest tightness, constant fatigue, faintness and light-headedness, feelings of panic, headaches, heart palpitations, insomnia, muscular aches, twitches or stiffness, tingling, numbness, and cold hands and face.

Some of these symptoms mimic heart attacks, so if in doubt, always go to the hospital or doctor to get your heart checked. The doctor always says to come back if you are unsure. I did this until I understood my stress patterns.

Controlled breathing is like this:
- Breathe in slowly through your nose for the count of 4.
- Hold it for about 2 seconds while you release your shoulders.
- Breathe out through your mouth while you count to 4.

While you breathe out, relax what you can, such as your stomach, jaw, and hands. Then, after getting used to this exercise, increase the count to 5, then 6, then up to 8 counts.

Look up alternate nostril breathing. It's fun!

The aim is to shift from upper chest breathing to abdominal breathing. So, while you breathe in slowly, have one hand on your chest and the other over your abdomen. That will connect you to how you breathe. This is your starting point.

That's the outcome we are going to achieve. At first, though, concentrating on our breathing can provoke panic and hyperventilation. If this keeps happening, try visualisation, such as happy places, yoga, massage, or just stretching. I tried having massages first, as I knew a lovely gentle masseur who understood my needs. She told me about the temporomandibular joint. Then I tried yoga. I usually love walking. It all helps relax the body.

A hint is to breathe out first. Then, the body will breathe in by itself. Try massaging your temporomandibular joint. This is your jaw, and a masseur once told me it is the most important joint in the whole body. That's interesting as it is the joint often most affected by stress. It took me a long time to release the tension in my jaw. At first, it was extremely painful and tight. It made my eyes water to touch my jaw. So go slowly and gently with this joint. But persist with it. It will be released over time. I also used a mouth guard at night to stop teeth grinding. A dentist got the mould of my bite, and then they made a little, lightweight plastic guard to put in each night. Don't use a sports mouthguard. They are too hard and don't serve the purpose of stopping teeth grinding.

Once you are into controlled breathing each day, there are physiological changes that occur in your body:
- Lowered blood pressure and heart rate.
- Reduced levels of stress hormones in the blood.
- Reduced lactic acid build-up in muscle tissue.
- Balanced levels of oxygen and carbon dioxide in the blood.
- Improved immune system functioning.
- Increased physical energy.
- Increased feelings of calm and well-being.

With enough practice, you can even use controlled breathing when you are in an anxious situation.

Emotional Release Work

Many emotions and actions are set off by our thoughts and interpretation of events, not by the events themselves.

Event > Thoughts > Emotions

Our emotions can also have a big effect on our thoughts about events.

Event > Emotion >Thoughts

Examining our thoughts and checking the facts can help us change our emotions.

1. Ask: What is the emotion I want to change?

Google emotions and check out the lists of emotions. Print off the list if it helps you to find your usual emotions. Ask: What is the event prompting my emotion? Describe the facts that you observed through your senses. Challenge judgements, absolutes, and black-and-white descriptions.

2. Ask: What are my interpretations, thoughts, and assumptions about the event?

Think of other possible interpretations. Practice looking at all sides of a situation and all points of view. Test your interpretations and assumptions to see if they fit the facts.

3. Ask: Am I assuming a threat?

Label the threat. Assess the probability that the threatening event will occur. Think of as many other possible outcomes as you can.

4. Ask: What's the catastrophe?

Imagine the catastrophe occurring. Imagine coping well with a catastrophe (through problem-solving, coping ahead, or radical acceptance).

5. Ask: Does my emotion and its intensity fit the facts?

Check out facts that fit each emotion. Examples of emotions that fit the facts are fear, anger, disgust, envy, jealousy, love, sadness, shame, grief, and guilt. For example, for guilt, your behaviour violates your values or moral code.

Ask Wise Mind. This DBT (Dialectical Behaviour Therapy) term means the mind that fits between the child's emotional mind and the adult's reasonable mind and embodies mindful thinking, intuition, and balance (Marsha M. Linehan, 2015).

Do opposite action (acting opposite to an emotion's action urge, such as instead of getting angry, think of compassion) and problem-solving.

The 40 to 5 Problem-Solving Technique

This technique is very useful.

1. Get an A4 piece of paper and a pen or pencil. Then, write the problem at the top of the page with your dominant hand.

2. Next, write fast, without thinking and using your subdominant hand, the problem in about 40 words.

3. Then, write it fast without thinking, using 20 words.

4. Then, write it fast in 10 words.

5. Then, write it fast in 5 words.

It's helpful to write with your subdominant hand, as this hand is the Royal Road to the Unconscious Mind, and it **tells the truth.** The five words are the key to the problem. Sometimes, the result of this method can blow your mind!

The first time I used this method was to understand the behaviours of a family member. For example, the heading might be "What is (name) agenda?" Try not to use "Why? Questions. They are more challenging to answer. Often, we don't know why someone does or doesn't do something.

Emotions – Types & Groupings

There are primary and secondary emotions. The primary ones connect to our core feelings, and we often do not let these feelings out. One of these may be loneliness. Since we struggle to express this feeling, we revert to the secondary emotions surrounding it. These might be low self-esteem, stress, anxiety, depression, or mistrust. For one lonely person, her secondary emotion may be low self-esteem. For another person, his secondary emotions may be mostly coldness and hostility. For a third person, her secondary emotions may be self-hatred. These are all personal patterns of the expressions of a hidden primary emotion under visible secondary emotions. When these coping patterns are chronic, they become 'emotional baggage' or distress that affects a person's life until they look at the baggage and unpack it. Then, they can get help with the primary emotion.

This can be terrifying at first, as the primary emotion has been held in the unconscious mind for many years. The reaction is to quickly bury it again, panicking all the while. We often need to tell someone we trust about this hidden primary emotion rather than look at it on our own. It comes back to needing to be **validated** again.

Here is a Template for exploring feelings/emotions:

- Right now, I am feeling …..

- This is because …..

- These feelings are really …. (Validate them)

- I have these feelings because ….. (Past stuff)

- Because of that, I tend to experience the feelings associated with that in the present (Validation)

- Even though right now I feel that …..

- I know these feelings will pass, and it is okay for me to feel them because of the events in my past.

These feelings were designed to keep us SAFE and preserve life. Now, with adult cognitive awareness, we can use neuroplasticity to retrain and change neuropathways in the present.

- Firstly, we sit with these feelings, validate them, and accept their IMPORTANCE.

- Secondly, we make mental notes of each event/trigger/feeling. Take these to therapy.

- Thirdly, once you have identified and talked a trigger out, it becomes disempowered and less likely to be a trigger in the future.

- Lastly, instead of reacting to that trigger, you can respond to it in mindful ways, such as breathing, walking away, or saying,

"No, that is just a reminder of a past trigger.

I don't get triggered by that … anymore."

Maslow's Hierarchy of Needs

Psychologist Abraham Maslow first wrote about the concept of a hierarchy of needs in 1943. It has since been so widely accepted and taught that it is still a handy tool for people to recognise where they still have deficits.

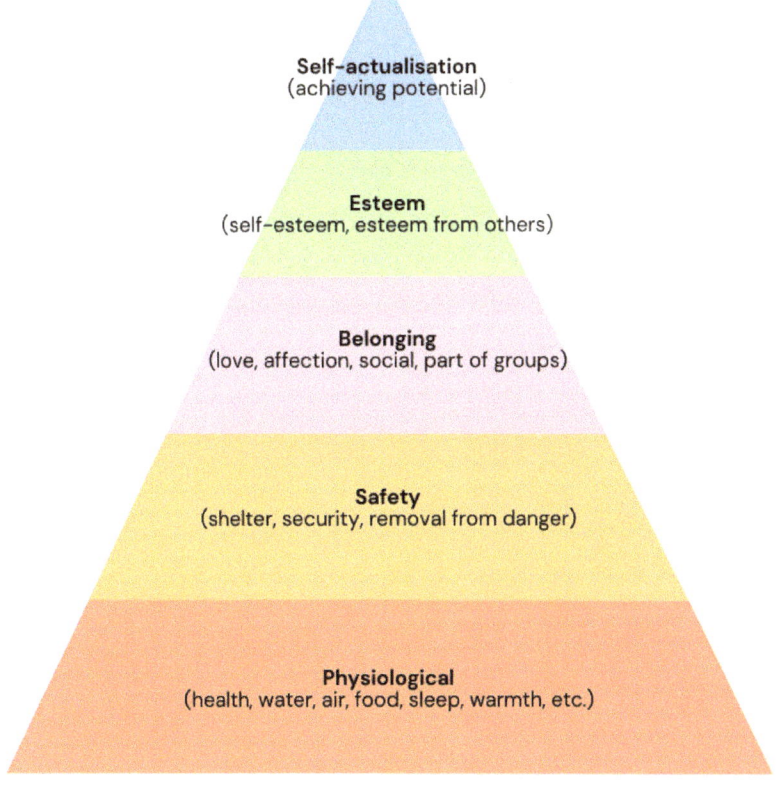

Maslow believed that physiological needs must be met before people can move on to higher needs. For instance, if a person is starving, this stops further growth.

However, life for an abused person is less clear. For example, if a child is unsafe at home but feels safe at school, that child may do well. If the child is also an extrovert, they may have many friends at school. On the other hand, introverts may be very shy at school even though they are good at their studies.

Remember, on p. 54; we discussed Core Needs underpinning Core Beliefs.

1. Secure attachment to others taps into Safety

2. Autonomy, competence, and a sense of identity taps into Safety and Belonging.

3. Freedom to express valid needs and emotions taps into belonging.

4. Spontaneity and play taps into Physiological and Safety.

5. Realistic limits, such as healthy boundaries and self-control, tap into belonging, esteem, and self-actualisation.

As you can see, these are slightly different from Maslow's Hierarchy of Needs because they cross into various levels. However, they do make more sense because they highlight the ways abused people can be stuck: with poor or no personal boundaries, no voice, no safe person or people with whom to talk things through, no or poor sense of identity, and/or no clear ideas of how attachments work.

Personal Boundaries

As we travel into Thriver Mode, checking and rechecking our boundaries is important. It takes a while to lock healthy personal boundaries into a comfortable sense of well-being, and it is worth the effort. It means that you can be comfortable wherever you are. For example, I like to choose a seat with my back to the wall rather than having my back to the door, as I want to keep an eye on who comes and goes. It feels safer to me. I have noticed that returned soldiers also do that. I do this wherever I am, such as in a library, café, or pub. I also like to be toward the end of a table of people I'm with rather than in the middle. I want to have a clear exit if needed. I always pick the seat on the back left-hand side of a taxi to watch the driver out of the corner of my eye.

Keep checking how far out you are comfortable with your boundaries. Then, adjust your distance when you are with someone else until you feel most comfortable. This taps into your feelings of Safety. Practise saying 'No' whenever you feel tired or unable to keep socialising at any point in your day. Everybody needs time out to recharge. This is healthy behaviour and essential to your sense of well-being and identity. It is assertive behaviour rather than aggressive.

Assertiveness

When we have developed our sense of identity and self-esteem, we can be assertive without being rude and aggressive. Remember in Chapter 7, pg. 85, how we talked about the Repeating Cycles that occur out of triggering events? One way trauma survivors react to triggers is by being aggressive. This is a natural response to an abnormal environment.

When we get to the point of turning aggressiveness into assertiveness, we are more able to express ourselves and our rights without violating the rights of others. Appropriately direct, open, and honest communication is self-enhancing and expressive. Being assertive allows us to feel confident and will generally gain us the respect of peers and friends. It can increase our chances for honest relationships and help us to feel better about ourselves and our self-control in everyday situations. This, in turn, will improve our decision-making ability and our chances of getting what we need from life.

However, before we can be assertive, we need to believe that we have a legitimate right to have those needs. This is the clincher. When we believe in our rights, we don't have to justify our position, be swayed by the opinions of others, or be passive and unassertive or reactive and aggressive. You can change your mind, tell others how you wish to be treated, ask for information or help, say "I don't know' or "I don't understand." make mistakes, and end a relationship if it doesn't meet your needs.

Assertiveness means the right to change, enhance, or develop your life however you determine. This is not selfish or aggressive; it is healthy behaviour.

Specifically, be clear and direct, own your message, and ask for feedback. This communication is both verbal and nonverbal—body language. To act assertively takes time, practice, and a willingness to accept yourself as you make mistakes. People who understand and care about you are your strongest assets, so practice with them.

Practise radical acceptance.

- Nothing is a waste of time.
- Observe that you are questioning reality.
- Remind yourself that the past, as unpleasant as it was, cannot be changed.

Realise that the future is yours to embrace.

- Cope ahead with events that seem unacceptable.
- Attend to body sensations as you think about what you need to accept.
- Allow disappointments, sadness, or grief to arise within you.
- Acknowledge that life can be worth living despite pain from the past.
- Do the pros and cons if you find yourself resisting practising acceptance, such as the following:

    A Thriver learns coping skills, turns scars into stars, has a beginner's mind, is encouraged by past experiences, can endure symptoms with relative comfort or acceptance, and perceives that one has moved beyond traumas.

The idea is: Don't let the bastards win.

You are the survivor who has managed to keep living. You are learning to thrive, and no one except yourself can take that away from you. You are also learning to sit with your new sense of self, which can feel like warmth and fuzziness in your heart centre.

This practice leads to assertiveness. We do not allow others to walk over us or treat us like dirt anymore. We have as much right as anybody else to stand our ground, walk the street, do our shopping, enjoy a coffee, or go to see the doctor.

According to Dr Caryn Aviv (TEDX):

1. We have choices, including "No."
2. We will be truthful and authentic *
3. We will ask directly for what we need.
4. We will rule out resentment by saying "No."
5. We will HONOUR our need for REST.
6. Not apologise for saying "No."
7. My/our integrity will not be compromised if I/we don't please others first.
8. We haven't lost our energy.
9. We have TIME – take it if we feel ambivalent.
10. We will say "Yes" ONLY when we mean it.
11. If others DON'T LIKE US BEING AUTHENTIC, then it's their stuff.
12. If we are not for ourselves, who will be?

This is how we grow courage—practice, practice, practice.

*TRUTH from point 2 above is tricky when we don't have anyone to validate our experiences. We can doubt our memories, nightmares, and flashbacks. I did. It all seemed so fanciful and weird. However, when I found someone professional whom I trusted with my truths, I learned that nightmares and flashbacks are not fanciful, especially when they recur again and again. They recur until we deal with them with someone we trust because that professional can help us get past the nightmares. One method I learned is to draw or write out the nightmare, then speak it out. This moves it from the limbic system towards the base of the brain and into the frontal lobe, and this process disempowers the nightmare and prevents it from happening again. The brain gives us nightmares until we work through them. Once we understand what the nightmares tell us, the brain stops having those nightmares.

Background Briefing on Radio National, Sunday, 14 November 2021, was about trauma. See if you can find the podcast. A trauma psychiatrist, a detective, and a trauma survivor were interviewed. The detective said he didn't realise that only 12% of childhood traumas are from strangers. He said that the police needed to change their beliefs and rules to incorporate all people a child knows as suspects in an abusive situation. I found it supported and enhanced my TRUTH.

Indigenous Australians are still struggling to express their truths. They try it at Reconciliation each year and sing it in music. I listen to Triple J. BlakOut, a cool hour of Indigenous music from 5 to 6 pm on Sundays.

Anyone who has been abused is part of a culture that abuses people. That's Australia and many other countries.

Creative Journaling

Here is where I'd like you to think of ways to journal your thoughts, nightmares, flashbacks, and panic attacks. It's important to have boundaries around these journaling times, such as when, where, and what to journal. For instance, you might like to journal before sleeping at night. This is a good time to journal as you can sleep soundly, knowing everything is written down. Nightmare fragments can be added as they occur.

If your time is not yours at home, you might try to journal in the car, library, beach, bush, or a café. Anywhere you feel safe is the idea.

The other thing to mention is the type of journaling that suits you. It may be written, art, mind dumps (as in fast writing without thinking about your writing), tabulated, collage, or cartoons. You may have another way of journaling. Pick a way that resonates with you. Make it a game to find your preferred way.

If you connect with colour, try oil pastels. These are pleasantly tactile, and the oil pastels get on your fingers, allowing you to use your fingers on the paper to smear or merge colours. They are also a way to represent emotions. If you feel a certain way but can't explain it, try colour to show the colours you feel. This way, drawing your emotions' colour can evoke the words that describe what you are going through, like opening the door to more awareness.

If you connect with the country, try picking up rocks, leaves, or bark representing your feelings. Then, it will be easier to talk about your feelings.

Visualisation

This is a valuable tool for helping you feel safe. It may be the place to go to do creative journaling. Visualise a safe place to escape when you need some time from stressors, whether therapy-related or day-to-day issues.

This can be a real place you remember from the past, such as a favourite, safe relative or friend's house. It may also be a favourite person, pet, beach, bush area, or garden in the present. Otherwise, think of an imagined place, such as one from a book or movie. For instance, I like to go to the beach in the movie 'Contact.' Sometimes, I go to the planet Mars.

Next, consider what things you need to take to the safe place that gives additional comfort. What colours are in this place? What sort of lighting is there? What needs to be in place to keep out unwanted intrusions? This may be a handle on your side of the place, barbed wire, or electric fences. Like me, you may be the only person there. I like to hear white noises in my head, so I sometimes use this place, especially at night when I sleep. I find it calming.

Having a Life While in Therapy

This revolves around hobbies, sports, social interactions, voluntary work, and pastimes like weeding the garden. Anything that creates a distraction from your healing journey is good. Distractions keep us in the present and mindful, and they provide pleasure. This raises the endorphin levels in the brain, which is why distractions feel so good. Look for humour and fun in your distractions.

At first, this may seem selfish, and you might feel guilty. This is ok. It just tells you you have some work to do on why you don't feel worthy. Pick a simple distraction, such as sipping a cup of tea while listening to music or listening to the birds singing outside. This will ease you into other distractions. It will also keep you hydrated! Regular hydration is necessary for good physical health. If you do nothing else, remember to hydrate and drink electrolytes to keep salt levels up.

Even gentle stretching is an excellent activity to do each day. You don't have to leave the house.

Paradigm Shifts Through Healing

These occur at different stages in our healing. One such stage shifts from "It's my fault. I am ashamed" to "It's not my fault. It's the abusers' shame."

To put this another way, when you were a child, where was your rational, adult mind and your own choice? Answer: you weren't adult or rational, nor did you have a choice. When you realise this truth, you realise that you've been had and learn to be blinkered from the truth. This is also how you survived.

Now we can shift our baggage and our fault to their crap and their fault. The paradigm shift is from a helpless child to an adult with choices. However, as adults, we need validation from others before we can accept the truth about our childhoods.

Another paradigm shift occurs when we realise how much of our life has been overshadowed by our abusive past. It's helpful to list how you have lived your life since childhood, such as being hypervigilant.

Survivor's behaviours:

Brain & D.H.A.

D.H.A., docosahexaenoic acid, is a long-chain polyunsaturated omega-3 fatty acid that benefits brain, eye, and heart health throughout life. For a complete list of products containing D.H.A., visit www.lifedha.com.

You may find other sites online. Natural D.H.A. comes from plants, such as the algae that fish eat. It's high in flaxseeds/linseeds at 1500 mg/day. If you prefer, you can buy Blackmores Flaxseed Oil at the chemist.

Then, add Vitamin D into the mix. Stand in the sun in the morning after you rise, eat mushrooms fresh after leaving them in the sun for half an hour, or eat seafood. Vitamin D absorbs calcium and promotes bone growth. Low vitamin D levels can cause muscle weakness, pain, fatigue, and depression.

Goal Setting

Many people feel adrift in the world. Covid-19 hasn't helped, and people are more wary. They are struggling to make an income to support their families and pay rent. They tend not to think about what they want from life. Even in hard times like these, we can learn about the process of setting goals to help us choose where we want to go in life or what we need in the immediate future.

Remember that goals must be **S.M.A.R.T.**

Specific - Often, we set goals that are not clearly defined, and then it's hard to know whether we hit the goal. A specific goal may be: I will go for a walk every day, weather permitting. This may be a walk around the block, to the end of your street, or to the letter box. Once you lock this habit in, it becomes easy to extend the walks.

Measurable - Spend 5 minutes each day writing in your diary. This might initiate a cup of tea and a sit-down. This sort of measure makes it easy to hit your goal.

Attainable - goals need to be reasonable and achievable. You will need the resources and time to carry out your goal. If you don't have the time or the money to accomplish your goal, you must select something else to work toward.

Relevant - goals must align with your values and beliefs and be something you want to carry out. Someone else cannot set this goal as it will not be personally meaningful, and you will not be motivated to achieve it. This will ensure you commit yourself to achieving the goal and taking responsibility for your efforts and outcomes.

Time-bound - If we don't set a time for a goal to be achieved, we are more likely to procrastinate and put it off. T can also stand for **T**angible – when we experience it with our senses.

We can have long-term and short-term goals. The longer-term goals are the big-picture ones, such as finding a new place to live. Short-term goals might be to get out of bed by ____:00 am or finish one household chore.

There are four domains in our lives in which we can set goals. These are love, play, work, and health.

Three steps to goal setting:

1. Create your "big picture" of what you want to do with your life, or over the next seven years, ten years, etc. and identify the large-scale goals you want to achieve.

2. Break these goals into smaller targets that must be hit to reach your lifetime goals.

3. Once you have your plan, start working on it to achieve these goals.

4. Be realistic—Re-set, review, re-set, review, re-set, review. Be gentle with yourself.

Make sure your goal is for something you want and sounds good for your soul, like soul food.

A goal cannot contradict any of your other goals. Develop goals in all areas of your life to aim for a balanced life, such as family, home, friends, financial, spiritual, physical, emotional, social, cultural, and educational. Write your goal in the positive instead of the negative.

Write your goal out in complete detail, taking your time over this. Make sure your goal is high enough. Go for the stars, and if you don't reach them, you will still be a better person out of your efforts. Shoot for the Moon!

Importantly, write down your goals. This becomes your roadmap to success. Then, review your goals regularly. If you need to change a goal, it is not a failure. You've learnt and can see things more clearly than when you started.

Then, check your daily decisions. Does this take me away from or closer to my goal? Visualise the completed goal each morning and each night. This will train your conscious and subconscious minds to work toward the goal. Once this happens, achieving your goal will become easier.

Management Plans

These can be daily, weekly, monthly, or yearly plans.

A daily plan includes grounding, safety, and self-soothing.

- Grounding - Using the five senses, such as listening to music or having tea with some chocolate or other favourite food. These help after you have experienced a stress response, such as a nightmare or flashback, or you have zoned out and become numb. Grounding helps bring you back to the present, whether you have woken in panic or been out and been triggered by something in the environment.

Name 5 things you can see,

5 things you can hear,

5 things you can smell.

- Safety - Communicating that you are not safe; using PRNs such as an anti-anxiety tablet; ringing a friend; ringing 1800Respect; or ringing for an appointment with your G.P.

- Self-soothing options include watching Netflix, a soft blanket around you, using noise-blocking headphones, or a cup of hot chocolate.

A **weekly plan** can include appointments and shopping.

A **monthly plan** can include social engagements or

booking ahead for things like a road trip.

A **yearly plan** can include car service, paying rates, school fees,

and booking a holiday.

BUILDING RESILIENCE

Human Declaration #10:
"I have the right to make mistakes. It is impossible to be perfect – therefore I do not have to try. I am human and fallible and therefore able to and do make mistakes. An honest mistake is a life experience I can learn from – not one that I must berate myself for or be punished for. I can simply acknowledge the mistake and carry on with living."

Healing Hints

These are from a friend I met along the way. They are procedures for dealing with body/mind issues or anything else at all. They are listed in order of doing, and the given is time - do this at your own pace. For instance, the initial drawing might be this week. Later, you may get to point 2, and so on. **Slower is faster.**

1. Drawing what you feel or think is less scary than writing, and often, it's hard to find the words to describe the issues.

2. Description of what you see without interpretation, e.g., black outline, down mouth.

3. Depiction of drawing with new understanding, e.g., down mouth says sadness and grief.

4. Listing keywords from the above.

5. A cluster of words with some kind of connection to each other. Then you can see the titles, like "Muscles" or "Pain," may recur.

6. Writing a poem or little song.

7. Writing fast without conscious/thinking input.

My friend said, "The body feels incredible grief and the amazing beauty of the land, sky in the day, and Cosmos at night."

Yin-Yang applications include this sort of thing. Grief and awe can occur together, fast and slow, upbeat and downbeat, rest and physical activity, healing work and art/craft/gardening/walking/swimming/coffee, sun and shade, and laughing and crying. I like to think 'Yin-Yang' daily. It's about getting a life balance. So, I've put the Yin-Yang symbol on the fridge to remind me to switch things regularly.

Learned Optimism

This is a term coined by Martin Seligman's research. He argues that we can cultivate a positive perspective and live with a glass half full rather than half empty. It's a matter of thinking positively rather than negatively.

Learned optimism is a concept that says we can change our attitude and behaviours by recognising and challenging our negative self-talk, among other things. It's a positive psychology concept that is the opposite of **learned helplessness:** a phenomenon whereby individuals believe they are incapable of changing their circumstances after repeatedly experiencing a stressful event. However, I beg to differ. I think that learned helplessness becomes involuntary and outside our consciousness after repeated abuses. Until someone shows you the term 'learned helplessness,' you don't even know how you have been made to feel.

Once we understand that we can change from learned helplessness to learned optimism, our health, well-being, and successes improve, and we start to feel that we have control back. We begin to use approach-focused methods for dealing with health issues, and we tend not to stress about things so much anymore. It's also about living in each moment. Planning stops procrastinating and putting things off. This frees up each moment and gives us things to look forward to. We now have goals locked in and feel motivated to fill each day with something enjoyable. This is freeing in all senses of the word. The body is more relaxed, we can breathe easier, have an internal locus of control, and feel optimistic about our world.

The **Attributional Style Questionnaire (ASQ)** is a self-report measure that helps us assess our explanatory styles and optimism. It is easily found online. Try it and see where you fit. It is an excellent starting point for changing your perspective.

The other aspect of learned optimism is cognitive distortions – the 3 P's.

1. Personalisation – an internal vs. external attribution style. If something terrible happens, a pessimist will attribute it to internal factors as their fault or failure. In contrast, an optimist will attribute it to external factors as someone else's fault.

2. Pervasiveness – the global or specific element of adversity or adverse event. A pessimist will say, "I did a terrible job. I'll never be hired again, EVER." Or "I'm unlovable again." An optimist will see an event as pervasive from the outside and try to avoid it. It is not my fault.

3. Permanence - whether we view a negative situation as fleeting or lasting and unchanging. For example, pessimists might say, "I'm always a bad dancer; I'll never be any good." An optimist may say, "I probably didn't dance so well because my leg is sore after I fell on it yesterday. I'll be back on top soon."

4. Look up the **Learned Optimism Test** (offered by Standard University). It's a 48-item test you can do online.

We can change our explanatory styles by challenging our cognitive distortions. Seligman introduced an adapted version of Dr. Albert Ellis' **ABC technique**.

The acronym ABC refers to:

Adversity – e.g., fighting with a friend

Beliefs – e.g., "I'm an awful friend and always will be."

Consequences - For example, you don't try to make peace with your friend because you can't change who you are.

Your explanatory style is how you get from A to B and then to C. Changing B will change C. If interested, google Albert Ellis' ABC Model or access Cognitive Distortions worksheets.

Being a Curious Explorer

Imagination helps with curiosity. It opens up alternative perspectives and leads to asking questions about an issue.

It is how we relate to our thoughts and feelings. **It's not about whether we pay attention but how we pay attention to what is happening in the present.**

Resisting our opposing craving for certainty, we discover that the greatest rewards come when we question authority, the status quo, our beliefs, and everything.

Following directions **conserves energy**, but following one's unique direction **expands energy**.

Non-judgement encourages CURIOSITY.

Instead of desperately trying to explain and control our world, we curious explorers see our lives as an enjoyable quest to discover, learn, and grow. We don't take positive events for granted; we investigate and explore them further.

Small, innocuous changes can enhance our days and lives. Baby steps every day encourage change, slowly and carefully. In this way, we change or modify our brains, enhancing our ability to flourish in a world with more unknowns than knowns.

There is a simple storyline for how curiosity is the engine of growth:
- By being curious, we explore.
- By exploring, we discover.
- When this is satisfying, we are more likely to repeat it.
- By repeating it, we develop competence and mastery.
- By developing competence and mastery, our knowledge and skills grow.

As our knowledge and skills grow, we stretch and expand who we are and our lives. The science of neuroplasticity now tells us that our personality is malleable and that we can become more (or less) curious.

We know that emotions last for seconds, moods last for hours or days, and our personality is something forged over the years since early childhood. If we want to change, we need to begin our work with each second, practising the mindset of a curious explorer. This will help change our brain in subtle ways, eventually weaving new strands into our personality.

We are constantly trying to balance the positive and negative. Our hardwiring to attend to the negative has a name – the **negativity bias.** This is our intense reaction to potential threats. This becomes generalised anxiety in which any ambiguous or uncertain situation is experienced as dangerous until proven otherwise. This negativity bias is best examined with a therapist because it is linked back with, usually, early traumas. There is also a **positivity offset** that means we feel safe. Then, we can explore new things, new thinking, and seek out new experiences. We get pulled towards rewards and excitement. Without this offset, we cannot learn, stretch, grow, or evolve as individuals.

Our curiosity and threat detection systems evolved together, and they function to ensure optimal decisions are made in an unpredictable, uncertain world. This is a fact. Therefore, it is about getting the balance between the two by working on our traumatic past to find out who we are first.

A trauma nurse once said,

"Sometimes we have to go over our limits to learn what they are."

Attune to your body and to the subtle signs and cues of pain, tension, and gut feeling. Be mindful. Imagine a bridge with stable, grounded towers at each end. In the middle are anxiety, hypo- or hyper-vigilance, and threats.

Underneath these is a safety net. The safety net consists of a woven net of skills, such as how to ground or problem-solving techniques. Even if we feel that we are falling into a black hole, there is a bottom to it. You can be stuck in the black hole for a while, but eventually, you can climb out using the skills you have learned in your pocket. Above the safety net is **resilience.**

Active listening & 'I' Messages

Communication is a two-way process in which sending a message is as important as hearing the message. It creates a feedback loop in which we can work to clarify any misinterpretations or difficulties in the communication process. Active listening is more complicated than we think. We not only hear the verbal message with facts or opinions but also recognise the other person's underlying feelings, wants, and needs.

Active listening is crucial because it:

- Creates an atmosphere of understanding by looking at issues from another's perspective.

- Lets the other person feel heard and validated.

- Gives time to consider the message and know the facts.

- Clarifies the situation for both parties.

- Does NOT mean agreeing or disagreeing but hearing and understanding the message.

Some questions to help you understand active listening:

How does the other person know they are being heard?

How does it make you feel when you know someone isn't listening?

What are the barriers to active listening?

How does this impact on you and your relationship with another person?

Listening in interpersonal conflict is most difficult, especially when you feel threatened and experience the flight, freeze, fight, and fawn response. So, use the following suggestions to listen more attentively in these difficult situations.

1. Act and think as a listener. Turn off any distractions (e.g., television, radio, computer), face the other person, and devote your whole attention to the other person.

2. Make sure you understand what the other person is saying and feeling. Use your active listening skills.

3. Express your support or empathy. You may say, "I can see where you are coming from." Or "I can see how what I said has upset you."

4. If appropriate, indicate your agreement, e.g., "You are right to feel upset in this situation."

5. State your thoughts and feelings as objectively as you can. Avoid criticism or blame.

6. Get ready to listen to the other person's responses to your statement.

Of course, this is tricky if you are the recipient of abuse because, quite often, the abuser refuses to admit to any fault or harm. This reaction shuts the door on any further communication.

'I' messages help to put this blame firmly where it belongs. You can say how you are feeling without mentioning blame. It enables you to own and describe your feelings in a clear, direct message. It feels like taking a considerable risk, so be aware of your boundaries and have an escape exit.

An 'I' message uses this formula:

I feel ....

(emotion/one word)

When you ....

(specific behaviour/FACT)

Because..

(effect on you/practical, interpretation, expectation)

I would like..

(specific behaviour/reinforce preference)

Some tips:

- "Emotion" needs to connect to the "Because".

- Pre-plan your "I would like" suggestions.

- Ensure you and the other person are comfortable, safe, and without distractions so your message can be heard.

- Lower your distress levels BEFORE you attempt communication.

- Practise the statement to yourself out loud to get the tone and facial expressions naturally and flexibly. Then, you may send your 'I' message successfully and respectfully.

You can keep yourself safe by using 'I' messages because you are not blaming the other person. You are explaining how their actions have made you feel. This is how to file a formal complaint against any injustice. Always write it in terms of the effects on you. This gets the attention of the authorities. It is SMART: Specific, Measurable, Attainable, Relevant, and Time-bound. This acronym also applies to goal setting (see below under "Putting meaning into your life".

Wisdom & Suffering

Wisdom is the attribute that allows us to discover what is right. Wisdom is the application of intelligence and emotion together to make moral decisions. Right or wrong do NOT exist in the realm of pure intellectual reason—they can only be illuminated by applying the heart and the mind.

Suffering is either internalised—making it their reason for being and shaping it into a dark reason to continue with vengeance—or externalised by accepting it and then seeking something else entirely. They search for ways to SOLVE it, to minimise the suffering of others, even if it requires them to suffer more themselves. It's the choices we make that determine our survival.

Be Inspired to Keep Changing/Growing

Think about a recent time in your life when you decided to make a change. Let's consider a personal change, such as starting an exercise regime, rather than a change that may have been chosen for you by somebody else.

1. What was the change that you decided to make?

2. Before deciding to change, what were the costs and benefits involved in making this change before you took any action towards changing?

List them in the table below, as this makes them easier to compare:

BENEFITS OF CHANGING	COSTS OF CHANGING

1. Did you notice anything difficult about making this change? What got in the way?

2. Did you notice anything easy or beneficial about making this change? What worked?

3. What makes change difficult?

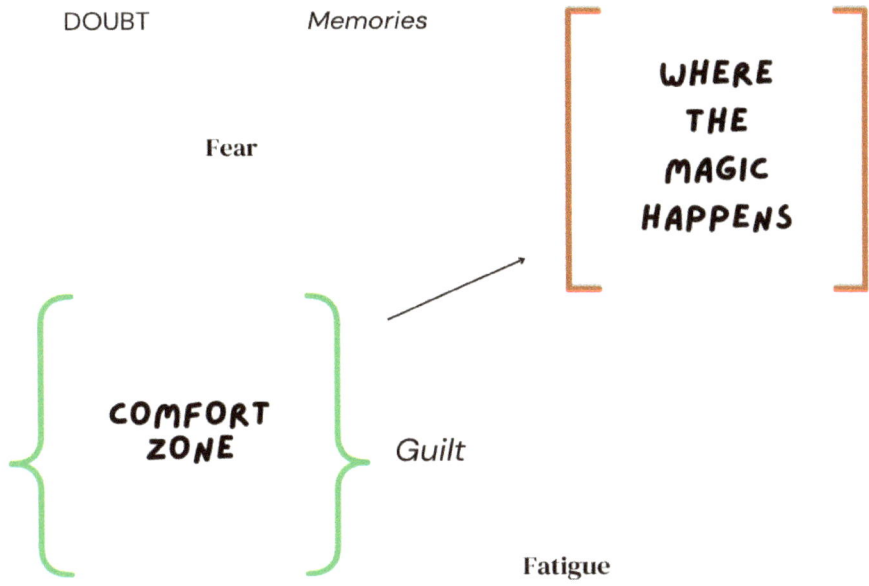

Cognitive distortions (e.g., "You'll fail" or "It's easier if you give up")

Feeling disorientated, anxious, or uncertain is a normal reaction to change. However, difficult thoughts and feelings can prevent us from making the changes we desire when they become overwhelming or cause us to lose sight of the "end goal".

Why we Might not Like Change: lessons from childhood

During childhood, we might have experienced feelings of not being safe. This then led to a craving for stability and safety or, during childhood, our parents worked hard to keep us safe from danger.

They might have done this by:

- Keeping us away from potentially difficult situations.
- Warning us about potential dangers.
- Praising us for being organised and predictable.

In these ways, our childhood experiences made us value stability, predictability, and certainty.

Uncertain, sudden, or unpredictable situations are perceived as dangerous or threatening. We feel anxious/out of control when we perceive a new situation as dangerous or threatening.

To avoid feeling anxious, we stop making changes so that our world remains stable and predictable. However, we can also feel stuck, and if so, this is an excellent time to reflect on that, as it may be the right time to make some minor changes in your life to test the waters.

While you are doing this, check out your thoughts, feelings, and sensations.

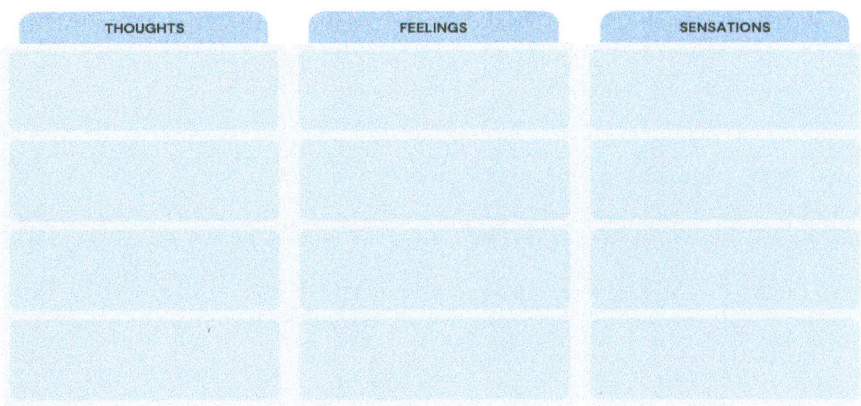

At first, changes tend to feel very uncomfortable if you've never changed anything before. That's a normal response.

Next, think about the costs and benefits of staying the same in any situation where change is a possibility.

Look carefully at what it costs you to remain in your comfort zone and stay the same. Here are some other reasons why it is a good idea to start thinking about ways to cope with change:

- Change is inevitable. Small changes occur constantly, which means it's not realistic to expect that everything will always stay the same.

- Not every change is a choice. Some changes are forced on us, such as being made redundant or the death of a loved pet or person.

- Learning to enact small changes can help us develop the ability to cope with uncertainty, which will assist us when change does come out of the blue.

However, change can still involve grief for what is lost or left behind. Google the Kübler-Ross Change Curve. Not every stage in change is necessarily felt. For example, we may not get depressed or feel shocked by a change. The curve is a way to see all the possible stages of change.

If you have unhelpful thoughts, challenge them because there will be a reason why they occur. The reason may be linked to a Core Belief, such as "I can't succeed in anything."

Next, here are hints to help you commit to change:

- **Keep your expectations realistic:** Maintaining an outward look but aiming for what is realistically attainable is helpful. Doing so ensures that the negatives won't be so devastating, and the positives will be an adrenaline rush.

- **Recognise your choices:** When change is thrust upon us, there is much we cannot control—or so it appears at first glance. Brainstorming and problem-solving can help us consider our choices. Over time, to implement the change, some of our choices will close. However, new ones will open. Always be aware of your choices because choice delivers control.

- **Expect bumps along the way:** Do not expect the change ahead or the change you are already experiencing to be pain-free. The world is imperfect, so it's realistic to anticipate dead ends, communication breakdowns, and misunderstandings despite our efforts to avoid them. Thus, factor in some setbacks in case they happen.

- **Not everyone will change at the same time.** Some people will adapt quickly, while others will take more time, and for others, the adjustment will be gradual.

- **The results (positive) of change may come more slowly than we would want.** Keep going if you have started your new exercise routine but have not noticed any changes. Keep plodding along. You can ask your GP or other professional for advice to ensure you are using appropriate exercises for your body.

- **Develop your own personal change tactics.** These may include plenty of rest, a type of hydration, a lean diet with plenty of fibre, or fast and slow exercises to break things up. When you experience confusion or are snowed under with the changes swirling around you, ask for help.

- **Acceptance:** Acknowledging that change involves difficult thoughts, feelings, and sensations and that it is often slower than we might like involves an element of acceptance. Accepting that change is a process with both positive and negative aspects can help reduce our aversion to the challenges that change can bring.

Lastly, remember the Basic Human Rights at the top of each chapter; know your Early Warning Signs of becoming overwhelmed; relax as you go rather than letting the stress/tension build-up; and think about your primary emotions, such as the anger volcano or the deeply depressed black hole.

Putting Meaning Into Your Life

What gives your life a sense of meaning or purpose? Are you living through your Core Values? Do you know your values by now? Your values are the foundation on which all your future planning, goal-setting, behaviour, and actions are built.

Let's break this down a bit more:

- Values are statements about what you want to be doing with your life, what you want to stand for, and how you want to behave on an ongoing basis.

- Values are our heart's deepest desires for how we want to interact with and relate to the world, other people, and ourselves. They are leading principles that can guide and motivate us as we move through life.

- Values are like a life compass that guides our lives and actions in the direction we want to go. They reflect what you want to do and how you want to do it. They guide your life choices. They represent how you want to behave towards yourself, your family and friends, your work, the wider community, and the environment.

- Values can be thought of or expressed as a statement or word.

- Values are in our heart-centred as love, desire, a quality of life that you gravitate to naturally, what you know to be true for you, what is most important to you, and what brings you joy, happiness, and peace.

At the top of this section, I mentioned 'goal setting' under Values. These are what we want to achieve along the way. For example, a value is like heading north; a goal is like a river, mountain, or valley we aim to cross while travelling north. Another example is the value of making your own clothes from materials you find in op shops; a goal is to learn the stitches and understand the process involved with making the clothes.

In other words, values are higher ideals that incorporate goals of how to go about it. If you don't know how to get to your value, that's ok. It means that your value is worthwhile. It just means that you need to do some research on how to reach a Value. Say you have the goal to get your children to school on time. This may mean that you value being a good parent.

Lastly, remember that goal setting needs to be **SMART**—Specific, Measurable, Attainable, Relevant, and Time-bound. This helps us reach our values.

Gratitude

Gratitude stems from the Latin "gratia", meaning grateful and pertaining to kindness and the beauty of giving and receiving. Gratitude is defined as being aware of and thankful for the good things that happen and taking time to express thanks. Practising gratitude is a simple and effective tool for building your happiness:

Because it reminds you of the positive things in your life. One positive thing about surviving traumas is that you are still alive. That, in itself, is amazing!

Because it turns bad things into good things. Traumas are bad, but they give us empathy and compassion for others who have experienced traumas. Other people struggling under the weight of past traumas know if someone like you talks with them. They pick up on the genuine nature of your words. This helps others to not feel so alone with their problems and addictions.

Because it reminds you of what's important. "Every day is a good day in the life of the Sun, without which we wouldn't be here." This is my daily motto. Also, try not to major on minor things such as forgetting to shop for essential items (there's something you can eat), the washing getting rained on (final rinse!), the dog walking muddy footprints through the house (the floor gets a wash); or the grass is too long (look for edible weeds).

Because it reminds you to thank others. People like being appreciated for who they are and what they do. It costs you little but makes someone else happy. Doing that helps your sense of happiness grow a little. Many others around you have suffered. They're trying to hide their pain as you have done. You can thank others who have helped you out of your pain by being there. It may be an animal that helps, like a dog or a horse. Or it may be a neighbour, GP, counsellor, or church group. Be open to help and try to go with your flow. That makes things easy because you are not fighting your flow.

You may like to take a photo each day of something you enjoy, like cloud patterns or a garden. You may like to stop at the end of each day and think about what you did, what you ate, who you saw, and where you went, or just three good things that happened yesterday. One good thing may be that you got out of bed and looked out the window. Keep it super simple.

Another helpful tool is to write a letter to someone who hurt you. You don't have to send it. It helps you to get past the hurt. You may find it helpful to write about the following things:

1. Why are you writing this letter?

2. What are you grateful for – be as specific as possible.

3. Describe the things you are thankful for in concrete terms.

4. Describe how their behaviour affected you, how you benefitted, and what you learnt.

5. Allow yourself to be in touch with the feeling of gratitude as you write.

6. Read and re-read the letter to ensure that it captures your thoughts and feelings.

7. Put it away, tear it up, or burn it.

People who abuse us are usually very young souls with basic needs. Millions of young souls exist in schools, churches, emergency services, armed forces, neighbourhoods, and governments. It feels better inside once you pick them out because it becomes a cultural problem rather than an individual problem.

The Royal Commission into Defence and Veteran Suicide opened on Monday, 29 November 2021. It was established on 8 July 2021 to inquire into systematic issues and risk factors related to harm. The final report is due by 15 June 2023. In fact, as of 10/03/24, it is still going.

If you are a veteran who was abused, contact the Royal Commission at royalcommission.gov.au.

It's very important to report your abuses as it helps with validation – that they believe you and that you are not alone.

Suppose other institutions in Australia have abused you. In that case, the Royal Commission into Institutional Abuses has closed, but '**KnowMore**' has lawyers and counsellors who helped at the Royal Commission. Now, it has gone private to keep the flow happening. They are supporting people who went to the Royal Commission and taking it further with people who went to the Royal Commission and are now seeking Redress. They are also accepting new applications. 'KnowMore' is a free, independent legal service providing advice to survivors of institutional child sexual abuse about justice and Redress. Advice line: 1800 605 762.

I am personally very grateful for the Royal Commission.

During this handbook, you will have noticed that it is divided into Victim, Survivor, and Thriver.

An explanation is now in order:

VICTIM	SURVIVOR	THRIVER
Helpless. Out of control. Angry. Hoping to be rescued. Perception of lacking choices. Self-pity. Passive. Payoffs (secondary gains). persuade person to remain in Victim role. Identify as a victim. In pain, numb. Defeated. Avoidance of feelings "I'm still in the trauma". Controlled by memories. Controlled by depression, anxiety, hatred, bitterness, revenge, and/or physical complaints. Has not yet learned from the experience, likely to repeat trauma, victimization. Shame. Self-dislike. Self-destruction. Addictions.	Satisfying sense of having gotten through intact or mostly intact. Beginning to feel strong. Perception that one has resources and choices. Recognition of one's potential to change and grow. Living one day at a time; coping from day to day; present time is primary focus. Beginning to take control. Beginning to "thaw out" or heal. Living moderately well. Suffering begins to lessen. Neutral about life – not depressed, but not happy. Realization that one is outside of the trauma; one has gotten through it. Extricated self from abuse (either in actuality or at least one has mentally triumphed over it).	Committed to move forward. Planning for the future. Active. Self-determined. Feels joy day to day. Achieving mastery. Self-esteem; sees self as more than a victim – a valuable person. Reaching out to others; finding meaning and purpose. Ennobled by the experience; has grown from the trauma. Living well. Can endure remaining PTSD symptoms with relative comfort or acceptance Guilt has been resolved. Generally satisfied with life. Perception that one has moved beyond trauma.

APPENDICES 11

Human Declaration #11:

"I have the right to feel good about myself – following on from Basic Human Right No. 1 – I have my own unique talents and abilities, self-worth, and human dignity. My self-worth is not determined by feelings, thoughts, or behaviours. It is mine by right of being a person. I therefore have the right to graciously accept compliments and share my good feelings of self-worth with others."

This chapter is divided into Guidelines on how to find professional therapists with healthy boundaries, A Recovery Bill of Rights, Dissociative Experiences Scale, References, and Resources (local and national).

Guidelines

Guidelines for finding a counsellor (therapist), Davis (1990).

- Are you trauma-informed?

- How do you describe PTSD; DID?

- Make sure they believe that you were abused. (Here we are looking for Validation)

- That they never minimise the experiences or the pain.

- Has or can get information about the HEALING PROCESS for abuse survivors.

- Is willing to hear and believe the worst experiences you have had.

- Keeps the focus on your experiences, not on your abusers.

- Doesn't push reconciliation or forgiveness.

- Doesn't want to have a friendship with you outside of counselling.

- Doesn't talk about their problems.

- Doesn't want to have a sexual relationship with you, ever.

- Fully respects your feelings (grief, anger, rage, sadness, despair, joy).

- Doesn't force you to do anything you don't want to do.

- Encourages you to build a support system outside of therapy.

- Encourages your contact with other survivors of child sexual abuse.

- Teaches you skills to take care of yourself.

- Is willing to discuss problems that occur in the therapy relationship.

Some other questions:

- Can we schedule extra sessions or call you during a crisis?

- Is a crisis call quick and straightforward to get me safe?

- Discuss fees.

- Discuss the professional boundaries of the therapist.

- How long are the sessions?

- Do you take phone calls during the session, and can I/we take important phone calls?

- Do you change my/our appointment times, or do I/we control them?

- Do you just fit me/us in between your other commitments, meaning that I/we wait when you get held up outside?

- How is the session closure handled/approached?

During therapy sessions:

- Pay attention to your gut feelings about the therapist. This is a reasonable basis for judgment.

- Do we feel listened to?

- Are we believed?

- Do I get a clear feeling the therapist likes us?

- Does the therapist believe in our capacity to heal?

- Does our therapist respect our ideas and points of view?

- Do we TRUST our therapist?

- Do they respect my/our boundaries?

- Do they respond well when I'm/we're in a crisis?

- Can I/we discuss problems in therapy?

- Does my/our therapist admit to making mistakes?

- Does my/our therapist help me/us to find my/our answers?

- Does my/our therapist encourage me/us to utilise other resources for healing (like this handbook)?

- Have I/we made progress since beginning therapy?

DON'T GO BACK IF:

- You felt like a specimen.

- You felt that the therapist was more interested in forming a friendship than in helping you work through the issues you came to therapy to work through.

- At any point, you are not listened to. This can be in the form of reflective listening. Good therapists will paraphrase what you say to make sure that they understand what you say. I like it when this happens because I know the therapist is listening, and I feel that what I say is validated.

Tools

A Recovery Bill of Rights for Trauma Survivors by Thomas V Maquire, Ph D (1995). At tmaquire@pipeline.com

As a Matter of Personal AUTHORITY,

You Have the Right...

- To manage your life according to your values and judgement.

- To direct your recovery, answerable to no one for your goals, effort, or progress.

- To gather information to make intelligent decisions about your recovery.

- To seek help from various sources, unhindered by demands for exclusivity.

- To decline help from anyone without having to justify the decision.

- To have faith in your self-restoration powers and seek allies who share it.

- To trust allies in healing as much as any adult can trust another, but no more.

- To be afraid and to avoid what frightens you.

- To decide for yourself whether, when, and where to confront your fear.

- To learn by experimenting, that is, to make mistakes.

For the Preservation of Personal BOUNDARIES,

You Have the Right...

- To be touched only with your permission, and only in ways that are comfortable.

- To choose to speak or remain silent about any topic at any moment.

- To choose to accept or decline feedback, suggestions, or interpretations.

- To ask for help in healing without accepting help with work, play, or love.

- To challenge any crossing of your boundaries.

- To take appropriate action to end any trespass that does not cease when challenged.

In the Sphere of Personal COMMUNICATION, You Have the Right...

- To ask for an explanation of communications, you need help understanding.

- To express a contrary view when you do understand and you disagree.

- To acknowledge your feelings without having to justify them as assertions of fact or actions affecting others.

- To ask for changes when your needs are not being met.

- To speak of your experience, with respect for your doubts and uncertainties.

- To resolve doubt without deferring to the views or wishes of anyone.

Specific to the DOMAIN of Psychotherapy, You Have the Right...

- To hire a therapist or counsellor as coach, not boss, of your recovery.

- To receive expert and faithful assistance in healing from your therapist.

- To be assured that your therapist will refuse to engage in any other relationship with you – business, social, or sexual – for life.

- To be secure against revelation of anything you have disclosed to your therapist, unless a court of law commands it.

- To have your therapist's undivided loyalty concerning any perpetrators, abusers, or oppressors.

- To receive informative answers to questions about your condition, your hopes for recovery, the goals and methods of treatment, and the therapist's qualifications.

- To have a strong interest by your therapist in your safety, with a readiness to use all legal means to neutralise an imminent threat to your life or someone else's.

- To have your therapist's commitment to you and not depend on your "good behaviour" unless criminal activity or ongoing threats to safety are involved.

- To reliably know the times of sessions and your therapist's availability, including, if you so desire, a commitment to work together for a set term.

- To telephone your therapist between regular scheduled sessions, if you are in urgent need, and have the call returned within a reasonable time.

- To be taught skills that lessen the risk of re-traumatisation:

>1. Containment (reliable temporal/spatial boundaries for recovery work)
>
>2. Systematic relaxation
>
>3. Control of attention and imagery (through trance or other techniques)

- To reasonable physical comfort during sessions.

Dissociative Experiences Scale -II (DES-II)

(Eve Bernstein Carlson, PhD, & Frank W. Putnam, M.D.)

Directions: This questionnaire consists of twenty-eight questions about experiences you may have in your daily life. We are interested in how often you have these experiences. However, it is important that your answers show how often these experiences happen to you when you are not under the influence of alcohol or drugs. To answer the questions, please determine to what degree the experience described in the question applies to you, then circle the number to show what percentage of the time you have the experience.

For example:

0%   10   20   30   40   50   60   70   80   90   100%

(Never)   (Always)

1. Some people have the experience of driving or riding in a car or bus or subway and suddenly realise that they don't remember what has happened during all or part of the trip. Circle a number to show what percentage of the time this happens to you.

0%   10   20   30   40   50   60   70   80   90   100%

2. Some people find that sometimes they are listening to someone talk, and they suddenly realise that they did not hear part or all of what was said. Circle a number to show what percentage of the time this happens to you.

0%   10   20   30   40   50   60   70   80   90   100%

3. Some people have the experience of finding themselves in a place without knowing how they got there. Circle a number to show what percentage of the time this happens to you.

0%   10   20   30   40   50   60   70   80   90   100%

4. Some people find themselves dressed in clothes that they don't remember putting on. Circle a number to show what percentage of the time this happens to you.

0%   10   20   30   40   50   60   70   80   90   100%

5. Some people experience finding new things among their belongings that they do not remember buying. Circle a number to show what percentage of the time this happens to you.

0%   10   20   30   40   50   60   70   80   90   100%

6. Some people sometimes find that people approach them that they do not know, who call them by another name or insist that they have met them before. Circle a number to show what percentage of the time this happens to you.

0%   10   20   30   40   50   60   70   80   90   100%

7. Some people sometimes have the experience of feeling as though they are standing next to themselves or watching themselves do something and they see themselves as if they were looking at another person. Circle a number to show what percentage of the time this happens to you.

0%   10   20   30   40   50   60   70   80   90   100%

8. Some people are told they sometimes do not recognise friends or family members. Circle a number to show what percentage of the time this happens to you.

0%   10   20   30   40   50   60   70   80   90   100%

9. Some people find that they have no memory for important events (for example, a wedding or graduation). Circle a number to show what percentage of the time this happens to you.

0%   10   20   30   40   50   60   70   80   90   100%

10. Some people experience being accused of lying when they do not think they have lied. Circle a number to show what percentage of the time this happens to you.

0%   10   20   30   40   50   60   70   80   90   100%

11. Some people experience looking in a mirror and not recognising themselves. Circle a number to show what percentage of the time this happens to you.

0%   10   20   30   40   50   60   70   80   90   100%

12. Some people have the experience of feeling that other people, objects, and the world around them are not real. Circle a number to show what percentage of the time this happens to you.

0%   10   20   30   40   50   60   70   80   90   100%

13. Some people feel that their bodies do not seem to belong to them. Circle a number to show what percentage of the time this happens to you.

0%   10   20   30   40   50   60   70   80   90   100%

14. Some people have the experience of sometimes remember a past event so vividly that they feel as if they were reliving that event. Circle a number to show what percentage of the time this happens to you.

0%   10   20   30   40   50   60   70   80   90   100%

15. Some people experience not being sure whether things that they remember happening really did happen or whether they just dreamed them. Circle a number to show what percentage of the time this happens to you.

0%   10   20   30   40   50   60   70   80   90   100%

16. Some people experience being in a familiar place but find it strange and unfamiliar. Circle a number to show what percentage of the time this happens to you.

0%   10   20   30   40   50   60   70   80   90   100%

17. Some people find that when watching television or a movie, they become so absorbed in the story that they are unaware of other events happening around them. Circle a number to show what percentage of the time this happens to you.

0%   10   20   30   40   50   60   70   80   90   100%

18. Some people find that they become so involved in a fantasy or daydream that it feels like it really happened to them. Circle a number to show what percentage of the time this happens to you.

0%   10   20   30   40   50   60   70   80   90   100%

19. Some people find that they sometimes can ignore pain. Circle a number to show what percentage of the time this happens to you.

0%   10   20   30   40   50   60   70   80   90   100%

20. Some people find that they sometimes sit staring off into space, thinking of nothing, and unaware of the passage of time. Circle a number to show what percentage of the time this happens to you.

0%   10   20   30   40   50   60   70   80   90   100%

21. Some people sometimes find that when they are alone, they talk out loud to themselves. Circle a number to show what percentage of the time this happens to you.

0%   10   20   30   40   50   60   70   80   90   100%

22. Some people find that in one situation, they may act so differently compared with another situation that they feel almost as if they were two different people. Circle a number to show what percentage of the time this happens to you.

0%   10   20   30   40   50   60   70   80   90   100%

23. Some people sometimes find that in certain situations, they can do things with amazing ease and spontaneity that would usually be difficult for them (for example, sports, work, social situations, etc.). Circle a number to show what percentage of the time this happens to you.

0%   10   20   30   40   50   60   70   80   90   100%

24. Some people sometimes need help remembering whether they have done something or have just thought about doing that thing (for example, not knowing whether they have just mailed a letter or have just thought about sending it). Circle a number to show what percentage of the time this happens to you.

0%   10   20   30   40   50   60   70   80   90   100%

25. Some people find evidence they have done things that they do not remember doing. Circle a number to show what percentage of the time this happens to you.

0%   10   20   30   40   50   60   70   80   90   100%

26. Some people find writings, drawings, or notes among their belongings that they must have done but cannot remember. Circle a number to show what percentage of the time this happens to you.

0%   10   20   30   40   50   60   70   80   90   100%

27. Some people sometimes find that they hear voices inside their heads that tell them to do things or comment on their actions. Circle a number to show what percentage of the time this happens to you.

0%   10   20   30   40   50   60   70   80   90   100%

28. Some people sometimes feel like they are looking at the world through a fog, so people and objects appear far away or unclear. Circle a number to show what percentage of the time this happens to you.

0%   10   20   30   40   50   60   70   80   90   100%

REFERENCES

Anndreopoulos, G. J. (1948). Universal Declaration of Human Rights. Encyclopaedia Britannica, 2 Jan. 2020. https://www.britannica.com/topic/Universal-Declaration-of-Human-Rights.

Bradshaw, J. (1994). Homecoming: reclaiming and healing your inner child. Ed. 1.

Davis, L. (1990). The Courage to Heal Workbook. HarperCollins Publishers, Inc. New York.

Kuhn, T.S. (1962). Edition 4. 2012. The Structure of Scientific Revolutions. The University of Chicago Press.

Linehan, M. M. (2015). DBT Skills training and Worksheets. Second edition.

Marra, T. (2005). DBT for Private Practice. New Harbinger Publications.

Middleton, W. (2005). Owning the past, claiming the present: perspectives on the treatment of dissociative patients. Australasian Psychiatry, 13 (1), 40-49.

Middleton, W. (2012). Boundaries and Boundary Violations. In: Encyclopaedia of trauma: an interdisciplinary guide. Ed. Charles R. Figley. SAGE Publications, Inc.

Mollon, P. (2002). Dark dimensions of multiple personality. In: Sinason, V. Ed. Attachment, Trauma, and multiplicity: Working with Dissociative Identity Disorder. East Sussex. Brunner-Routledge, 177-194.

Ogden, P. & Fisher, J. (2014). Sensorimotor psychotherapy: Interventions for trauma and attachment. New York. W. W. Norton.

Oksana, C. (2001). A safe Passage to Healing: A guide for survivors of Ritual Abuse. Backinprint, Lincoln.

Pease, A. and B. (2007). The Definitive Book of Body Language. Pease International Pty Ltd; HarperCollins Publishers Pty Ltd.

Ross, C. A., & Halpern, N. (2009). Trauma Model Therapy. A treatment approach for trauma, dissociation, and complex comorbidity. Maintou Communications. 1st Edition.

RESOURCES

National resources include the following. Add any others you come across or which come up as new Resources.

- Aboriginal Business and other Corporations.

- General Practitioner, such as how to access a Mental Health Care Plan

- Belmont Private Hospital, 1220 Creek Rd, Carina Heights QLD, 07 3398 0111

- Robina Private Hospital, (Sister hospital to Belmont PH) 1 Bayberry Ln, Robina QLD 4226, 07 5665 5100

- St John of God Midland Public Hospital, 1 Clayton St, Midland, WA 6056, 08 9462 4000. There are other St John of God hospitals in WA and another new one is being built.

- Look up St John of God Hospitals online. There are many that are offering mental health services, such as Burwood – 02 9715 9200 and Richmond – 02 4570 6100

- Austin Health – Psychological Trauma Recovery Service Outpatient services: 03 9496 2537; ptrsadmin@austin.org.au

- St John of God, Pinelodge Clinic, 1480 Heatherton Rd, Dandenong, VIC, 3175, 03 8793 9333

- Ramsay Clinic Cairns – Private Mental Health, 253 – 257 Sheridan St Cairns, QLD, 07 4050 7000

24/7 Services:

- Rape & Domestic Violence Services Australia Inc: 1800RESPECT counsellors

- Lifeline
- AA, NA
- Suicide Call Back Service
- Abnon
- Al - Anon
- Men's Line
- Men's Sheds

- Grow – Peer support group
- Beyond Blue
- Blue Knot
- Sane
- National Debt Helpline
- Centrelink

Local resources include:

- Local Neighbourhood/Community Centres
- CWA
- Meetup.com (social groups)
- Local councils for information on resources and activities
- Library

LOCAL SERVICES IN YOUR AREA

(Community Centre/GP Listings):

ACKNOWLEDGEMENTS

Firstly, we need to acknowledge the Trauma and Dissociation Unit (TDU) at Belmont Private Hospital, 1220 Creek Rd, Carina Heights, QLD, 4152, for all their guidance, group work, information sessions, support when needed, and validation. We have kept many handouts given out for TDU Inpatients and Day Programmes, and this information is used in the handbook. Other sources will be acknowledged; references are either in-text or in the Reference List.

TDU was founded by Professor Warwick Middleton, and we thank him for this. It saved our lives, being the last port of call after many failed attempts to find professional therapeutic help in regional Australia. This chronic lack of regional help is the reason for this handbook.

FROM THE PUBLISHER

In 'Handbook for Trauma Survivors,' Myra Adams bravely delves into the labyrinth of trauma with a vulnerability that pierces through the veil of silence surrounding dissociative identity disorder (DID) and complex traumas. With poignant prose and unflinching honesty, Myra invites readers into the intricate web of their own experiences, offering a guiding light through the darkest corridors of the mind.

'Handbook for Trauma Survivors' is a hands-on approach to healing, offering practical strategies and tools for managing the aftermath of trauma, from coping with nightmares and flashbacks to rebuilding a shattered sense of self. Moreover, Myra's candid advice on finding the right therapist underscores the importance of establishing a safe and supportive therapeutic relationship—a crucial step on the path to recovery.

I would like to take this opportunity to congratulate Myra on their unwavering courage and compassionate wisdom, offering hope, healing, and the promise of a brighter tomorrow for every reader. It has been a joy to work on this publication and I wish Myra all the very best.

Crystal Leonardi
Bowerbird Publishing
www.crystalleonardi.com

Myra Abrams

www.ingramcontent.com/pod-product-compliance
Lightning Source LLC
Chambersburg PA
CBHW061736070526
44585CB00024B/2697